The perseverance, commitment and sheer drive by the authors is inspiring. Steve and Kathie's odyssey of detective work in solving the first Great Lakes maritime mystery is impressive to say the least!

— *Stewart Berry, MBA – Former CMO AT&T Canada*

The possibility of discovery is exceptionally mind blowing ...

—*Robert McKeown*

LE GRIFFON
AND THE
HURON ISLANDS

1679

Kathie Libert — *Steve Libert*

Published by Mission Point Press
2554 Chandler Rd.
Traverse City, MI 49696
(231) 421-9513
www.MissionPointPress.com

ISBN: 978-1-954786-19-6 (hardcover)
ISBN: 978-1-954786-20-2 (softcover)

Library of Congress Control Number: 2021906839

Photos, title page: David Ruck

Printed in the United States of America

LE GRIFFON AND THE
HURON ISLANDS *1679*

Steve and Kathie Libert
Great Lakes Exploration Group, LLC

MISSION POINT PRESS

About the Authors

Steve and Kathie love history, adventure, and mysteries. Meeting in high school in Dayton, Ohio, they immediately realized they had these interests and many others in common. After college and marriage, Steve continued his childhood interest in his search for Robert La Salle's ship *Le Griffon* and convinced Kathie to take part. Complementing each other with their unique skills and research techniques, they discovered that together they made a great team. Steve, a retired senior intelligence analyst for the Chief of Naval Operations (CNO) and Kathie's entrepreneurial experience in owning her own business in marketing communications, made a perfect match for success.

Kathie and Steve Libert

A gifted researcher, Steve has over 42 years of experience researching legends and Great Lakes mysteries. His expertise in underwater technology and adventurous spirit in high-risk adventures such as wreck diving, offered him the opportunity to participate in many historical endeavors. His underwater expeditions and missions have taken him on journeys that only a few others have dared to undertake: to the East China Sea, Okinawa, Exumas, Florida's Keys, and his beloved Great Lakes. He has acted as consultant to the late, renowned author Clive Cussler as NUMA's Virginia Director; the distinguished archaeologist Dr. Lee Spence on the confederate submarine *CSS Hunley;* and the late, legendary shipwreck researcher Robert (Bob) Fleming. Steve has directly participated and/or shared his knowledge and expertise in projects such as the Titanic, I-52 submarine, Navy Flight 19 Avengers, Bon Homme Richard, the vessel of John Paul Jones, General Tomoyuki Yamashita's hidden troves, the Poverty Island Mystery, sinking of the Carl D. Bradley, missing L-39C *Albatross* and his life long quest, *Le Griffon*.

> *"He is, if nothing else, a masterful and dogged researcher."*
>
> Stephen Dina
> *The Washington Times*

Steve has appeared on various national and international media venues such as ABC's "Good Morning America" and "Good Morning Canada" along with Paris and NPR radio and newsprint. He has conducted many presentations throughout the Great Lakes region.

Kathie's keen sense for business and creative background led to the establishment of a highly successful brand marketing firm in the Washington D.C. metro area. She managed high profile Fortune 100 brands such as Mobil, ExxonMobil, and Lockheed Martin. Clients included business-to-business and business-to-consumers in high-tech, retail, energy, government contracting and non-profit industries. Her creative designs and clear, concise messaging gave credence to her strategic marketing plans that helped build corporate brands and solidified her success in marketing communications. Her creative team produced marketing materials, digital platforms and exhibits, including apps and videos. She was one of the first pioneers in the field of desktop publishing. Kathie's artistic background includes plein air painting, graphic design, illustrations, marketing and music. She has exhibited her artwork throughout several galleries in Virginia and Michigan.

Steve received his BA in Political Science with a minor in Economics in 1980 from Wright State University, Dayton, Ohio. Kathie received her BFA (Bachelor of Fine Arts) with a minor in Biology in 1978 from Wright State University, Dayton, Ohio.

They both reside in Charlevoix, Michigan.

Le Griffon and the Huron Islands

ACKNOWLEDGMENTS

We would like to acknowledge all the dedicated work and commitment to **The La Salle–Griffon Project** by individuals around the Great Lakes region and throughout the world. Without their passion for discovery, love of the Great Lakes, and unfaltering perseverance through difficult times and good times, this quest in search of the historical ship, *Le Griffon*, would not have been possible. The members of Great Lakes Exploration Group, LLC (**GLX**) are extremely grateful for this dedication and support. We would also like to extend our appreciation to explorers worldwide who seek to **IMAGINE** the possibilities — **EXPLORE** outside their comfort zones — and who venture to **DISCOVER** for enlightenment and preservation of our unique history.

This project would not have been possible without the love and support from our family and friends. Special thanks to Jennifer Carroll as contributing editor and Doug Weaver and his team at Mission Point Press for their guidance.

We dedicate this book to Pam, and to those loved ones who have left us.

Table of Contents

Preface

By Steve Libert

I was an eighth grader in Dayton, Ohio, when I first became intrigued by the mystery of a ship called the *Griffin*, in French *Le Griffon*. The story my history teacher proceeded to tell immediately caught my full attention and like most young men, stirred the imagination of early exploration in an unknown country. Fifty-one years later, I am still intrigued by this story. Exploration or seeking answers to the unknown seems to be seeded in our DNA; or at least in mine. I was intrigued by the mysterious disappearance of this ship — the flagship of explorer René-Robert Cavelier, Sieur de La Salle. **Le Griffon disappeared in 1679 on its maiden voyage — the first upper-decked vessel known to have sailed above Niagara Falls and into the upper Great Lakes.** Unknown to La Salle, the loss of his ship and six crewmen would begin a legend filled with mystique and a search that would continue over 340 years. For me, my interest began the day my teacher reached over and touched my shoulder and said out loud in class, *"Maybe one day someone in this class will find it."*

According to early historians, shipwrights and modern day researchers, *Le Griffon* was approximately 40 to 45 tons and 35 to 70 feet long. The ship was built by La Salle and his men in the wilderness on the banks of the upper Niagara River, two leagues above the great Falls of Niagara at the mouth of the Cayuga Creek to be specific. They had no shipyard and the area was surrounded by the Sonnontouans (Seneca Indians) who were in awe of the French for having built such a large canoe. These natives were also concerned for their safety, so much that the Sonnontouans tried to burn the ship during construction. The men had to launch the ship before completion to protect the vessel and themselves from danger, then rigged its masts and sails while on the river. My first thought was to imagine how this ship may have looked. Although there are many historical details to consider, the key to figuring out this mystery is to understand La Salle's shipwright, Moïse Hillaret and 17th century shipbuilding during La Salle's time of exploration. This was not an easy task, and historians, including myself, seemed to have his or her own opinions on the subject. The lack of clear, distinctive information led to various deductions. Kathie was instrumental in solving the most important and complex issue presented before us: finding the location of the ship. As a team, we worked closely together in writing this book.

In identifying this ship, three main factors were considered — confirming the correct geographic location of the sinking was first and foremost. The second was determining the building methods used in 17th century French ship construction, and thirdly, locating and identifying supportive cultural materials. In consideration of colonial ship construction, it's important to note that once *Le Griffon* was lost, there was a span of almost 100 years before ships resumed sailing the upper Great Lakes. By then, English shipwrights were designing ships that were completely different and more modern. *Le Griffon*'s hull design would be of an era long past, and would present itself as an early colonial ship revealing the ingenuity required to construct such a vessel in the wilderness,

Cover Photo:
Keelson & Frames
Possible *Le Griffon?*

Photo by Steve Libert

absent a well-equipped shipyard. Hillaret also had considerable knowledge of the difficulties of navigation they would encounter, especially the shoal waters and rapid areas in the Niagara and the St. Clair rivers. *Le Griffon's* hull construction and design was possibly constructed to address these challenges, a mystery of great interest to many shipwrights and historians.

The purpose of this book is to reveal the location of the Huron Islands where *Le Griffon* met its fate and to announce the exciting *discovery* of a colonial-age shipwreck, precisely where historical documents place *Le Griffon's* final moments. It was among these islands where, in 1679, Robert La Salle's flagship *Le Griffon* disappeared. Ironically, if this ship is *Le Griffon*, she has laid quietly under tribal waters for more than 340 years. Utilizing primary source documents, Kathie and I will take you on a historical journey of exploration and discovery to solve one of the first maritime mysteries of the Great Lakes.

> *"The historical significance of this flagship and her mysterious disappearance ignited a larger than life legend — inspiring many to seek answers."*
>
> —Steve Libert

Chapter 1

Introduction
Our Story of Exploration and Discovery

One of the most intriguing maritime mysteries surrounding Great Lakes lore is the disappearance of the first European vessel to sail west of Niagara Falls. *Le Griffon* (Griffin in English) was the first upper-decked vessel of size to sail lakes Erie, Huron, and Michigan, and the first ship to be lost in those waters as well. Built in the wilderness above the falls by the legendary French explorer, René-Robert Cavelier, Sieur de La Salle, *Le Griffon* was intended to carry

Wreck site debris field shows plenty of remains to consider in identifying the wreckage.

out lucrative fur-trading commerce which would support his expedition in search of the mouth of the Mississippi for King Louis XIV. On its maiden voyage, September 18, 1679, *Le Griffon*, loaded with 6,000 pounds of furs, sailed out from present-day Washington Harbor on Washington Island, never to be seen again. The monetary loss of cargo and six crewmen would be a devastating setback to La Salle's exploration, and ultimately cease ship navigation on Lake Michigan for almost one hundred years. Canoes and small flat-bottomed boats became the favored form of transportation for fur traders and miners, paddling close to shore for safety. La Salle would go on to claim the heart of the continent, over two-thirds of present-day United States, and he named it Louisiana in honor of the Sun King Louis XIV. In 1803, President Thomas Jefferson authorized Robert Livingston and James Monroe to sign the Louisiana Purchase Treaty. This land acquisition would double the size of the United States and eventually lead to America becoming a world economic superpower stretching from coast to coast.

La Salle not only left a legacy of claiming the Louisiana territory for France, he would also leave us the first and greatest Great Lakes maritime mystery of all time to solve. The loss of his ship, *Le Griffon,* on its maiden voyage, would lead to it becoming one of the most sought after ships in the world. Researchers and historians have searched for this elusive ship in hopes of solving the mystery surrounding its disappearance. With dozens of unsubstantiated claims to her discovery, *Le Griffon* seems eager to ply the waters once more. Many maritime enthusiasts are patiently waiting for this mythical creature to magically raise her eagle head and lioness body from the depths and continue along with her voyage. We believe we have uncovered the vital clues that solve this maritime mystery, exposing the facts that have been surrounded by decades of misinformation. Through primary source documents, and vintage maps and charts, we reveal the location of the legendary Huron Islands that initiated our lifelong quest in search of this fabled vessel. What unfolds next is the possible 2018 discovery of what appears to be a colonial-age wreck site. Could this be *Le Griffon*'s final resting place?

We had been researching the loss of *Le Griffon* since 1979. Our story of exploration and discovery began with the first dive in our search for *Le Griffon* on September 10, 1983, after uncovering the location of the Huron Islands. Summer vacations were eventually spent up north with two colleagues, Jim and Tom Kucharsky, seasoned professional divers, who, with the same drive for exploration, would become life-long friends. Brother-in-law Vance Skowronski would later join us for surface support. Our first major find of wreckage was in 2001 with the discovery of what appeared to be a bowsprit protruding from the bottom. Remote sensing showed wreckage buried beneath. We were hoping it was part of the ship. We applied for permits in 2003 to identify the site, but the State of Michigan denied the permits. Expecting further issues, we had created a private entity called the Great Lakes Exploration Group, LLC (**GLX**). The permitting process is where our story becomes complicated by the many years of enduring legal and political struggles with the United States government and the State of Michigan. To move the permitting process forward, we worked to secure moral support from the country of France and two Native American tribes. It was mentally and monetarily exhausting. Most sensible people would have quit. We were young and naive, expecting cooperation from government when, in fact, quitting was exactly what they wanted us to do. They even attempted to confiscate our research and proprietary information. We learned quickly that private entities are discouraged from conducting explorations of any kind, whether you have qualified expert archaeologists on board or not. We were operating in unknown territory, but continued to push forward to obtain the required federal and state permits needed to legally resume identifying the timber believed to be a bowsprit.

In 2011, Great Lakes Exploration Group eventually received assistance from our Michigan State Representative, Greg MacMaster, and the French DRASSM team (Department of Underwater and Submarine Archaeological Research). Both agreed to assist Great Lakes Exploration Group's goals to explore and identify our shared heritage. After ten years of perseverance, this undertaking would require the State of Michigan to finally provide us the necessary permits.

The alliance established the first international and interdisciplinary research team to commence test excavations on Lake Michigan bottomlands. Great Lakes Exploration Group formed the friendship project **The La Salle–Griffon Project** and moved forward with the 2013 expedition. Our accomplishments earned the Great Lakes Exploration Group official recognition by Michigan's former governor, Rick Snyder, and Michigan's U.S. Congressman, the Honorable Dan Benishek. Great Lakes Exploration Group would formally be recognized for our work in discovering and preserving the maritime history of the State of Michigan. Unfortunately, just a few years later, we would apply for two other test excavation permits and both were denied by the State of Michigan.

In lieu of this setback, **The La Salle–Griffon Project** continues to be recognized publicly, gathering interest throughout the country while encouraging academia and private businesses to participate in these historic endeavors. We continue to team up with subject matter experts in the fields of archaeology, history, underwater remote sensing and colonial-age ship construction in accomplishing our goals. Brian Abbott, president of Abbott Underwater Acoustics, LLC, is one of the subject matter experts, utilizing non-intrusive remote sensing technologies to gather images and data of the wreck and debris field. These images are at the end of the book. Abbott is recognized as a worldwide expert in the field of remote sensing. One of his most notable accomplishments is his sector scan imaging on the Titanic Mapping II Project.

Our discovery of 2018 appears to be a colonial-aged wreck site precisely where our many years of research places *Le Griffon*'s final moments. The unsuccessful attempts to secure the necessary permits from the State of Michigan left us with little recourse in identifying the wreck. We firmly believe the site warrants a thorough investigation by academia and France's DRASSM team. This book is our attempt to initiate the next steps for this identification and, at the very least, determine the wreck site's historical significance. We are not concerned with being ridiculed by releasing our story. There is an abundance of evidence both direct and circumstantial outlined in this book that supports a high probability that the wreck could indeed be Robert La Salle's ship.

Aerial view of the Huron Islands from Fairport, Michigan.
Photo by Eagle Eye Drone Service, Kewadin, Michigan

Aerial view of Fairport, Michigan.
Photo by Eagle Eye Drone Service, Kewadin, Michigan

The Use of the Word "Savage" in Historical Documents

In the 1600s, the Americas were populated with millions of flourishing indigenous people. Robert La Salle befriended the natives and traded among their people in a peaceful way. However, the continued unrest caused by the Iroquois War between North American tribes presented an uneasy and untrusting environment for La Salle and his men. You will see evidence of this in some of his writings. La Salle refers to the natives by their tribe names in his manuscripts and letters, but in many cases he and the Jesuits refer to them as "savages," a commonly used derogatory term, as they considered the natives uncivilized by European standards. Some of the excerpts in this book utilize the uncomfortable terminology. Early explorers understood the natives had their own governments, wars, politics, language, culture, art, medicine, and religion. Intermarrying among the French explorers, fur traders, and native people was common. Those who shared Native American and French heritage were called Metis; their knowledge of both native and French Great Lakes culture made them crucial to the operation of the Great Lakes fur trade from the early 1700s through mid-1800s. At its peak, fur trading was among the primary economic ventures in North America.

If the discovery is determined not to be that of *Le Griffon*, it will certainly add to another Great Lakes mystery. Historical and maritime entries records no other ship of significant age having been lost among the Huron Islands other than La Salle's elusive *Griffon*.

Our story invites you on a magnificent journey of discovery, a journey that is still unfolding. As explorers, we seek answers to questions that enrich the world around us. We believe the information in this book will answer many of your questions. It is our hope the discovery of the location of the Huron Islands alone will excite you.

After all, for 342 years these islands have held the secret resting place of the **Holy Grail** *of the Great Lakes, Robert La Salle's* **Le Griffon.**

Why we believe this is *Le Griffon*

In determining the identification of the wreck site, there are several filters of historical data we have outlined in this book. We list 8-CLUES gleaned from primary source documents, charts, and maps, allowing you to follow our rigorous journey to discovery. The final declaring moment was the actual discovery of a colonial-aged shipwreck scattered on the bottomlands, precisely where primary source documents indicated. Our book reveals the following vital information:

- The location of the Huron Islands;

- A Navigational Path of *Le Griffon's* maiden voyage to her demise;

- Historical documents infer the French knew the area where *Le Griffon* disappeared;

- The discovery of a colonial-aged shipwreck with uniquely French design features. The wreck, when reconstructed, presents a colonial-aged ship structure typical during *Le Griffon's* time; and

- Maritime history on the upper Great Lakes tells us the only ship of significant age would be that of Robert La Salle's *Le Griffon*.

In late fall of 2018, our assessment of the wreck convinced us that the site warranted further investigation. We engaged shipwright and shipwreck interpreter Allen Pertner, utilizing his expertise in delivering a final report and analysis of the wreck site. Pertner has over 60 years of shipbuilding experience and historical knowledge of ship construction. He provided us with an illustrated reconstruction of the ship, based on the limited data collected to date from the actual hull and frames. This book contains these exclusive illustrations and our photos of the wreck site captured during our very first underwater dive in cold, clear waters during the summer of 2018. This was no doubt a historic occasion and the most exhilarating and breathtaking moment of our entire lives. We are extremely humble and grateful to share them with you.

La Salle's ship would carry no large cache of gold nor jewels, and its bounty of fur is long gone, but this elusive ship mysteriously disappeared and left an intriguing legend that captured the hearts and imaginations of many. With a desire to preserve our early history, maybe it's time for a new chapter to be written for La Salle's elusive *Griffon,* in hopes of uncovering the true story of her disappearance and solving the most intriguing maritime mystery of the Great Lakes.

> *"It's not a treasure ship unless you consider*
> *history a treasure, which I do."*

> —Steve Libert, July 28, 2008
> ABC's "Good Morning America"

Father Hennepin:

> *... we went two leagues above the great Fall of Niagara, where we made a dock for building the ship we wanted for our Voyage. This was the most convenient place we could pitch upon, being upon a River which falls into the Straight between the Lake Erie and the great Fall of Niagara. The 26th, the keel of the ship and some other pieces being ready, M. de la Salle sent the Master Carpenter to desire me to drive in the first pin; but my profession obliging me to decline that Honour, he did it himself...*

> *... The ship was call'd the Griffon, alluding to the Arms of Count Frontenac, which have two Griffons for Supporters; and besides, M. la Salle us'd to say of this ship, while yet upon the stocks, that he would make the Griffon fly above the Ravens. We fir'd three guns, and sung Te Deum, which was attended with loud acclamations of joy; of which those of the Iroquese, who were accidentally present at this ceremony, were also partakers; for we gave them some brandy to drink, as well as to our men, who immediately quitted their cabins of rinds of trees, and hang'd their hammocks under the deck of the ship, there to lie with more security than a-shoar.*

> (*A New Discovery of a Vast Country in America* Father Louis Hennepin who accompanied La Salle on his journey.)

Chapter 2

La Salle
The Grand Expedition
Early North American Exploration, 1679

French Explorer René-Robert Cavelier, Sieur de La Salle was born November 22, 1643, in Rouen, Normandy, France. When he was a young man, La Salle had a choice of living a life as a Norman merchant like his father or choosing an adventurous calling of a missionary. The Jesuits were known to explore places like China, India, and the Americas to convert and discover new territories. Like every other explorer during the 17th century, La Salle aspired to the glory of finding the Northwest Passage to China. This was his passion, so he left his family's inheritance and worldly possessions to pronounce his first Jesuit vows at the age of sixteen.

La Salle spent the next four years in seminary studying navigational theory, geography, and cartography. He became skilled in many languages that would later help him master native dialects while exploring North America. He eventually became restless, and at the age of twenty-three found himself more attracted to adventure and exploration than his studies. When his request for a foreign mission was denied, La Salle decided to leave France and the seminary.

La Salle looked to Canada as an opportunity to develop the colony of New France. His elder brother, Jean Cavelier, was a priest and already living in Canada when La Salle decided to join him in 1667. Shortly after he arrived, La Salle received a land grant along the Saint Lawrence River from the Superior General of the Sulpician priests in Montreal. After establishing his new settlement on present day Montreal Island, which he named La Chine, La Salle was befriended by several Iroquois Indians who told him stories about a "beautiful river" which extended from the area just south of the Great Lakes to the sea. La Salle wondered if this could be the long sought-after Northwest Passage explorers hoped to find during their exploration of North America. Discovering this route would fulfill his dream. In 1669, within three years of arriving in Canada, La Salle accompanied the first expedition to begin exploring the western side of New York, the upper Great Lakes area, and he may have wandered as far south as the Ohio River. Then, in 1673, reports from his colleagues French Jesuit Father Jacques Marquette and explorer Louis Joliet convinced him that the Mississippi flowed not to the Pacific — meaning no Northwest Passage — but instead went south to the Gulf of Mexico. Marquette and Joliet were also looking for a northern route through the Americas to reach the Orient. With no clear route to China, La Salle set his sights on expanding the colony of New France.

Backed by Governor Frontenac of New France and supported by the King of France, La Salle petitioned and received Letters of Patent on May 13, 1675 (Figure 13, page 41), to fortify and secure Fort Frontenac at present-day Kingston, Ontario, as a base for colonizing the Mississippi Valley. La Salle had envisioned a chain of French forts stretching from the Atlantic to the Gulf that would channel the lucrative fur trade of the interior to France. He petitioned to the King again, who agreed to his second request to explore the western part of New France (Mississippi's watershed area), and granted Letters of Patent on May 12th, 1678, (Figure 13, page 41) on the condition that he complete the exploration of the Mississippi River within five years. La Salle had requested twenty years. Minister Jean-Baptiste Colbert, a French politician serving as the Minister of Finances for France from 1661 to 1683, also supported La Salle and asked him to establish a post at the mouth of the Mississippi River in order to prevent England from establishing a foothold in the heart of North America. Colbert's desire was to protect and secure the economy of New France.

In 1678, La Salle led the first party of Europeans to Niagara Falls and camped by the Niagara River. He was sent by Governor Frontenac and accompanied by three priests, including Father Louis Hennepin. Hennepin, who was the first to publicize the grandeur of the falls in his 1679 manuscript "A New Discovery of a Vast Country in America." In 1679, La Salle would construct his ship in the wilderness above the great falls and launch *Le Griffon* five months later in early May.

They're never weary of making new Discoveries. They're indefatigable in rambling through unknown Countries and Kingdoms not mention'd in History; leaving their minds with the Satisfaction of gratifying and enriching the World with something unheard of ... in order to satisfy their natural Curiosity, and inform their Minds.

—Father Louis Hennepin on Explorers

LA SALLE'S 1679-80 EXPLORATION

NEW FRANCE, CANADA

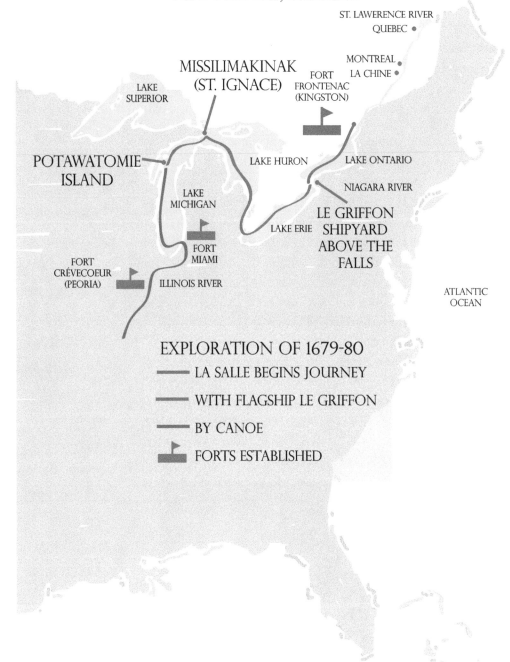

ST. LAWERENCE RIVER
QUEBEC •

MONTREAL •
LA CHINE •

MISSILIMAKINAK
(ST. IGNACE)

FORT
FRONTENAC
(KINGSTON)

LAKE
SUPERIOR

POTAWATOMIE
ISLAND

LAKE HURON

LAKE ONTARIO

NIAGARA RIVER

LAKE
MICHIGAN

LE GRIFFON
SHIPYARD
ABOVE THE
FALLS

FORT
MIAMI

LAKE ERIE

FORT
CRÉVECOEUR
(PEORIA)

ILLINOIS RIVER

ATLANTIC
OCEAN

EXPLORATION OF 1679-80

LA SALLE BEGINS JOURNEY

WITH FLAGSHIP LE GRIFFON

BY CANOE

FORTS ESTABLISHED

This ship was the first decked vessel to sail the upper Great Lakes of a scale and design in keeping with 17th century shipbuilding. Hennepin mentioned that La Salle named the flagship in honor of Count Frontenac, whose coat of arms was ornamented with the mythical creature with the body of a lion and the head and wings of an eagle.

Woodcut of Niagara Falls from Hennepin's "A New Discovery of a Vast Country in America."

Le Griffon disappeared on September 18, 1679, on her return maiden voyage from Lake Michigan, and with the loss of six men on board. It was devastating and costly to La Salle's mission; however, determined, he would quickly continue his quest to explore. His explorations would take him from Montreal, up the St. Lawrence River to the Great Lakes; from Lake Michigan to the Illinois River; and down the Mississippi River to the Gulf of Mexico where, in 1682, he finally explored the Mississippi Delta. While the English were isolated along the East Coast, La Salle ventured into the very heart of North America, down the "Great River" Mississippi, connecting Canada to the Gulf of Mexico by way of the Great Lakes — an amazing accomplishment.

After his successful explorations of the Mississippi Delta, La Salle returned to France to obtain support for establishing a southern fortified trading post at the mouth of the Mississippi River and the Gulf of Mexico. He left France on July 24, 1684, for the Gulf of Mexico with 180 colonists in four ships. La Salle was to arrive at the mouth of the Mississippi; however, he overshot his destination and was shipwrecked on Matagorda Bay, not far from present day Houston, Texas. Three years later, this ill-fated mission to start a French colony failed, and on March 19, 1687, at age 43, mutinous soldiers ambushed and killed La Salle at present day Huntsville, Texas.

During La Salle's explorations, he would face many challenges, including having to defend his own marriage as his business partners were concerned it would take away his focus on his mission. He had many people to answer to, which couldn't have been easy in accomplishing his goals. It was well known that he believed the Jesuits interfered with his men, instigating them to desert his enterprise and steal his goods. He would also claim the Jesuits interfered in his relationship with the Indians, trying to convince them that La Salle was their enemy. Early explorers like La Salle, who had much to lose and many enemies, would face insurmountable obstacles throughout their expeditions.

La Salle's Legacy

During La Salle's North American explorations, he went on to claim extensive lands in North America for King Louis XIV, a portion of which became The Louisiana Purchase. One hundred twenty-four years later, on Saturday, April 30, 1803, the Louisiana Purchase Treaty was signed by Robert Livingston, James Monroe and Barbé Marbois in Paris. President Thomas Jefferson announced the treaty to the American people that July 4. After the signing, Livingston made this famous statement: "We have lived long, but this is the noblest work of our whole lives… From this day the United States take their place among the powers of the first rank." (*America's Louisiana Purchase: Noble Bargain, Difficult Journey.*) America never looked back.

Le Griffon and its Elusive Place in History

La Salle also left another legacy. The legend and mysterious disappearance of his flagship *Le Griffon*. *Le Griffon* is one of the most sought-after shipwrecks in American history. This elusive ship has captivated the imaginations of modern day sailors, historians, and archaeologists alike, all wanting a part of its discovery and the chance to study and rewrite history. La Salle's *Le Griffon* became the first sailing ship to spread its sails on lakes Erie, Huron and Michigan, exciting the deepest emotions of the local Indian tribes occupying the shores of these inland waters. The saga of this ship's fate became not only one of America's early seafaring legends, but an enticing mystery to adventurers and historians since the news of its loss. La Salle would be the first to search for his lost ship, but to no avail. The elusive *Le Griffon* would be one of the most significant underwater archaeological finds in all of North America.

> *We went two Leagues above the great Fall of Niagara, where we made a Dock Building the Ship we wanted for our Voyage.*
>
> —Father Louis Hennepin

On August 7, 1679, La Salle set sail on *Le Griffon*. The expedition began at the building site of *Le Griffon*, near the mouth of Cayuga Creek where it flows into the Niagara River and Lake Ontario. La Salle then sailed his ship *Le Griffon* into Lake Erie, then Lake Huron to Missilimakinak (present-day St. Ignace, at the Straits of Mackinac in Michigan), before finally reaching the islands that line the entrance to Green Bay, Wisconsin. In September, La Salle dispatched a crew of five and his pilot Luc to sail *Le Griffon* back to Niagara, loaded with some 6,000 pounds of furs to pay off creditors, while he would continue his journey south by canoe. The crew of *Le Griffon* was to dispense its furs and return to meet La Salle at the lower part of Lake Michigan, near the mouth of the St. Joseph River.

Le Griffon sailed out of Washington Harbor on today's Washington Island on September 18, 1679. Father Hennepin, the Franciscan Recollect friar who had accompanied La Salle on the expedition, records the ship fired a single cannon shot as it set sail. Hennepin states that those on the land did not know which way the ship sailed after she left the harbor. *Le Griffon* would disappear entirely, never to be seen again.

The Mystery Continues

From this point on, there are plenty of rumors and speculations, but so far history has been silent. One theory is that Indians captured the crew, burned the ship and took the furs. There is little evidence for this; however, La Salle himself came to believe that the pilot and crew had mutinied, stolen the furs, and scuttled the ship to hide the crime.

Perhaps the most likely reason is that the ship was lost during one of the storms that frequent the Great Lakes during this time of year. It is known that there was a tremendous storm on September 19th, the day after *Le Griffon* left Washington Harbor. The ship may very well have sunk in that storm.

Kathie and I have spent years researching and studying the history of *Le Griffon*. We concentrated our focus tracking down primary source documents, always looking for one important clue — the whereabouts of the Huron Islands, the location where our research suggests *Le Griffon* met its fate on its maiden voyage.

We reveal the historical data that confirms the location of these islands and what initiated our 40-year search for this elusive ship. I started camping on the islands in 1983, and scheduling yearly dive trips with my colleagues. Diving around these islands gave me a key understanding of the area's underwater currents, storm patterns, and local shipwreck history. It was of great advantage to know the location of where a ship would shelter safely from a storm, or anchor when winds were blowing in from different directions among these islands.

Navigation by early explorers has always been a major interest for me. It's no surprise that La Salle had schooling in navigational theory, geography, and cartography. As a former senior intelligence analyst for the federal government, I am well experienced in navigational practices, so it was interesting to read what La Salle wrote of his own navigational knowledge of the Great Lakes through his explorations:

La Salle's Navigation Notes ('Lake of the Illinois' is present day Lake Michigan):

The River Niagara is not navigable for a distance of ten leagues from the Falls to the entrance to Lake Erie, it being impossible to take a barque up unless one has a sufficient number of men to keep it sailing, to pull it with tow-ropes and to wasp [warp] It at the same time, and even then with such great care, that one cannot expect to succeed always.

The entrance to Lake Erie is so obstructed by sand banks that, if a vessel is not to be hazarded every voyage, it must be left in a stream which is six leagues further on in the lake, there being no harbour nor anchorage nearer the end.

In Lake Erie there are three great headlands, two of which project more than ten leagues into the lake; there are sand banks on which one runs aground before seeing them if great care is not taken.

There is a change of direction to enter the strait, which leads from Lake Erie to Lake Huron, where there is deeper water and a strong current; there is great difficulty at the strait of Missilimakinac in entering the Lake of the Illinois from Lake Huron. The current there is usually contrary to the direction of the wind, and the channel narrow on account of banks which stretch

Woodcut of the Griffon - *Unknown.*

*out into it from both sides; no anchorage, or very little in Lake Huron, and no harbors there, any more than in the Lake of the Illinois, towards the North, West and South, a number of islands in both, — dangerous in the **Lake of the Illinois on account of the sandbanks in the offing.** That lake is not very deep and is liable to terrible storms, with no shelter, and the banks prevent one from approaching the islands; but it may be that, with more frequent navigation, the difficulties will be lessened and the ports and harbors become better known, as happened in the case of Lake Frontenac, the navigation of which is now safe and easy.*

(Journey of M. de La Salle to the River Mississippi. 1680)
(Navigation of the Lakes – Geographical Information from Ministere des Colonies.
Amerique du Nord. Enterprises de Cavelier de la Salle C 13 Vol. 3. Fol.33.)

After the loss of La Salle's ship, *Le Griffon,* navigation on the Great Lakes seemed uncertain and La Salle's partners questioned him about its safety. They wondered whether traversing the Ohio River would be safer than the lakes, using canoes for transportation rather than a barque as large as *Le Griffon.* La Salle found himself defending the barque over the canoe, and for good reason. La Salle mentions in one of his letters how necessary the barque is for the success of his enterprise. The fact is, he needed a barque to complete his enterprise, especially to have protection for his men.

Using canoes meant sleeping unprotected at night in the wilderness where enemies could attack versus sleeping in a hull of a ship. La Salle termed the barque as being a "fort" to get his message across:

La Salle:

> For they were obliged to encamp in the woods, where these savages are particularly skilled in surprises, **whereas a barque is like a fort** and provides a remedy for all these difficulties; and without using one this enterprise cannot possibly attain success, at least by this route.
> (The French called the Ohio River "Bauraond," the Iroquois called it Ohio.)

Hennepin also referred to *Le Griffon* in his document *A New Discovery of a Vast Country in America* as a "floating fortress":

Father Hennepin:

> The Iroquois being return'd from Hunting Beavers, were mightily surpriz'd to see our Ship a-float, and call'd us **Otkon**, that is in their Language, Most penetrating Wits: For they could not apprehend how in so short a time we had been able to build so great a Ship… **It might have been indeed call'd a floating Fortress;** for all the Savages inhabiting the Banks of those Lakes and Rivers I have mention'd, for five hundred Leagues together, were fill'd with Fear as well as Admiration when they saw it.

La Salle's partners also became concerned about sailing the lakes for navigation. Six-man canoes would take too long to accomplish La Salle's goals. A barque carried more men and larger cargo to its destination more quickly. Canoes could not carry the weight of the supplies he needed to build his forts and the iron needed for another barque. La Salle responds to one of his partners concerning a letter from his agent in Paris, Abbé Claude Bernou, commenting about mapping the navigable waters of the lakes and Ohio River using a canoe rather than a barque. Below is La Salle's reply:

La Salle:

> I think it impossible to do what the Abbé Bernou wrote to me about, — to send and ascertain whether the lakes and the great river were navigable, otherwise than by a barque. The latter has to keep a course very different from that of the canoes, which are obliged always to go as near to the shore as they possibly can in order to land as soon as the wind rises, for they could not withstand the slightest squall in the midst of these lakes, forty to fifty leagues broad; while barques cannot keep to far out, so that they may not be driven on shore. Hence it is necessary to go in a barque in order to discover the difficulties of navigation; or else indeed we must censure those who have crossed unknown seas for not having first tried them with their boats in order not to risk their ships.

Even if that had been possible, a period of three years would have been required to go all round the lakes, a distance of more than fifteen hundred leagues, where the slightest wind stops a canoe and one place for eight, ten, fifteen, and sometimes twenty days without advancing;

"The barque was absolutely necessary, and cannot be dispensed with for this enterprise…"

La Salle had only five years to explore the new world according to his Letters of Patent by the King of France. Remember, he had asked for twenty years to complete this task, so a canoe for transportation was definitely not going to meet his needs.

Luc the Pilot

With the loss of his flagship and crew, La Salle was devastated not only by what was lost in provisions, food, and supplies, but also the materials for building another ship necessary to explore the Mississippi River. A little information gleaned from La Salle and Hennepin's writings offers us some insight into the personality of the hired pilot for the expedition. Primary sources tell us his name was Luc, Luke, or Lucas. La Salle had brought him to the Great Lakes in 1678 because he had experience sailing on the largest vessels trading to Canada and the Caribbean. Luc was known for his temperament, and for not getting along with the crew. His stubbornness would cost the lives of the crew and the loss of La Salle's ship. He was a skilled pilot, but in his short employment had previously lost two of La Salle's barques. This was a considerable financial loss to the expedition. La Salle becomes aware of his pilot's negligence while sailing *Le Griffon* along Lake Erie's coastline when he almost wrecked upon a sandbar on their way to Missilimakinak. La Salle took over his ship and began to believe his pilot was in the pay of his enemies.

The following excerpts describe Luc and his temperament from La Salle and Hennepin's point of view.

La Salle:

Some Indians, called Pouteatamis, tell me that two days after the vessel left the island where I had quitted here on the 18th of September 1679, this storm arose, of which I have told you: **and the pilot, who had anchored with them on the northern coast, where they were encamped, believing the wind to be favorable for going to Missilimakinak, as in fact it was out in the lake, set sail contrary to their advice,** *not perceiving the violence of the wind because the land over which it blew was so near. They assured him that there was a great tempest in the offing, where the lake seemed all white:* **but the pilot laughed at them, replying that his vessel was not afraid of the wind, and set sail.** *The wind increased very much, and they observed that* **he was obliged to furl all his**

sails except two large ones: and after that, the barque could not keep a straight course, but drove obliquely towards some islands in the offing blocked by great sand banks, *which extend outwards more than two leagues. Then the wind became still more violent, with very heavy rain and they lost sight of the vessel. Nothing was heard of it until the spring, when two pairs of linen breeches, spoiled with pitch and all torn, were found on the coast: and finally, this summer, they found a hatchway, a bit of cordage and some packets of beaver-skin, all spoiled. All this made them believe that the barque had run aground somewhere on these islands, and was lost with all that was in it.*

(La Salle's letter sent to his agent Abbé Claude Bernou in Paris on September 29, 1680)

Father Hennepin:

The Ship came to an Anchor to the North of the Lake of the Illinois, where she was seen by some Savages, who told us that **they advised our Men to sail along the Coast, and not towards the middle of the Lake, because of the Sands that make the Navigation dangerous** *when there is any high Wind.* **Our Pilot, as I said before, was dissatisfy'd, and would steer as he pleas'd, without hearkining to the Advice of the Savages,** *who, generally speaking, have more Sense than the Europeans think at first; but the Ship was hardly a league from the Coast, when it was toss'd up by a violent Storm in such a manner, that our Men were never heard of since; and it is suppos'd that the Ship struck upon a Sand, and was there bury'd.*

(A New Discovery of a Vast Country in America)

Earlier, on this same upbound trip on Lake Huron, the crew had encountered a fierce storm that almost wrecked the ship. La Salle thought for sure they were going to perish.

Father Hennepin:

We sounded all Night long, because our Pilot, though a very understanding Man, was somewhat negligent.

M. de la Salle, notwithstanding he was a Courageous Man, began to fear, and told us we were undone; and therefore **everybody fell upon his Knees to say his Prayers, and prepare himself for Death, except our Pilot, whom we could never oblige to pray; and he did nothing all that while but curse and swear against M. de la Salle,** *who, as he said, had brought him thither* **to make him perish in a nasty Lake, and lose the Glory** *he had acquir'd by his long and happy Navigations on the Ocean.*

La Salle had to deal with strong personalities making his mission more dangerous. His own assertive personality was derived out of his strong will to accomplish his goals in such a short timeline, making one understand the type of person it takes to be an early explorer.

"It's more like looking

for a needle in a hay field."

— Steve Libert

Chapter 3

2013 Expedition — Site 20UM723, the Bowsprit
Overview of **The La Salle–Griffon Project**

Our first major expedition was one for the history books. Great Lakes Exploration Group's 2013 Expedition was initiated by our research that led to the discovery of an underwater structure officially known as archaeological site 20UM723. In June 2001, during an underwater exploratory dive with poor visibility, I bumped into what I believed was a bowsprit or a ship's mast while searching in our targeted area. It would

June 18, 2013 Expedition - Image of Bowsprit.

be the first "real find" of the discovery. Twelve years later, in 2013, we were able to move forward after receiving a long awaited permit from the State of Michigan. It took ten years of litigation and political wrangling in order to conduct a test excavation of the site. Great Lakes Exploration Group formed a friendship project with the French DRASSM team and its director archaeologist Michel L'Hour. We called the project **The La Salle–Griffon Project.** This undertaking would be one of the first expeditions to serve as a model for international and interdisciplinary research and underwater community archaeology. An international team of American and French archaeologists, professional divers from Great Lakes Diving and Salvage led by Tommy Gouin, and skilled recreational divers participated in the test excavation.

The 2013 Expedition was highly publicized for many reasons, one being the international involvement of the French DRASSM team. Secondly, the State of Michigan rarely gives out permits. Thirdly, the admiralty arrest of the bowsprit and permit process went through the court system, allowing journalists to keep the public aware of the arrest and our progress. When the permit was finally granted by the State of Michigan, we sent out a press release on our historic public-private agreement between a foreign sovereign nation, a state of the U.S., and a private exploration group. This was of great interest and importance to the private sector and gained worldwide recognition. An overview of the press release and project follows:

PRESS RELEASE: Great Lakes Exploration Group, France and Michigan Establish Cooperative Agreement for Shipwreck Exploration

MCLEAN, VA - 2010 - Great Lakes Exploration Group, the State of Michigan, and the Republic of France announced today that they have reached an historic agreement for cooperating in a Phase 2 archaeological site assessment for identifying what may be the site of a 331-year-old shipwreck at the bottom of Lake Michigan.

Shipwreck explorer Steve Libert, president of Great Lakes Exploration, discovered the site while diving in northern Lake Michigan in the summer of 2001. In the interim six years, Great Lakes Exploration has engaged in discussions and litigation with the State of Michigan, which claims exclusive ownership of the bottomlands of Lake Michigan. In 2008, at the request of Great Lakes Exploration, the U.S. Court of Appeals for the Sixth Circuit directed the District Court of Western Michigan to proceed with the arrest of the vessel, which created federal admiralty jurisdiction.

The agreement, which represents a unique partnership between a foreign sovereign nation, a state of the U.S. and a private exploration group, allows assessment to proceed of what Libert believes may be the final resting place of Le Griffon (English: Griffin), the first decked European-built ship to sail the upper Great Lakes.

The U.S. District Court for the Western District of Michigan will continue to provide protection to the site. It's expected that the U.S. Marshal will also continue to play a role in protecting the heritage of the site.

"It has always been the aim of Great Lakes Exploration Group to preserve the scientific, cultural and historical values of this site. We're pleased to have established an historic agreement for a unique public-private partnership in exploring and preserving our shared heritage. We believe we're on the verge of important archaeological and historical discoveries which will enrich our understanding of our history and culture," says Libert.

Overview of **The La Salle-Griffon Project**
Preparing for the 2013 Expedition

In 2004, **GLX** filed a Complaint, No. 1:04-CV-375 in the United States District Court for the Western District of Michigan and sought an arrest of an unidentified sunken vessel which may be the wreck of *Le Griffon*, a French naval auxiliary sailing vessel built in 1679 for the expedition of René-Robert Cavelier, Sieur de La Salle. *Le Griffon* is historically documented to have sunk during its maiden voyage and is believed to have sunk in the vicinity of site 20UM723.

GLX, Michigan and France agreed that an archaeological investigation is necessary to examine the Site to seek to determine the extent and identity of vessel remains and/or contents at the Site, with a view to determining whether the vessel is *Le Griffon* and the property of France. **GLX**, Michigan and France agreed that such a study may be conducted by **GLX**.

France has submitted a legal claim asserting ownership of *Le Griffon* as a vessel constructed for and engaged in the service of France at the time it sank and a vessel of great historical importance. France has advised the Court and the parties that, in the event that the Site is *Le Griffon*, France desires that it be studied and preserved for the public benefit, including archaeological and historical study, recovery, conservation, and display in the United States as a reflection of the cultural and historical heritage embodied by *Le Griffon*, with due recognition of **GLX** as discoverer. The State of Michigan, after consultations with France, has notified the Court that it does not object to the claim of ownership of France as to *Le Griffon*.

GLX agrees that, if the vessel is *Le Griffon*, it is the property of France and appropriate for study and preservation for the public interest in recognition of the cultural and historical heritage embodied by *Le Griffon*.

GLX agreed to manage and conduct site investigations in accordance with appropriate professional and scientific archaeological standards including the Standards of Research Performance of the Register of Professional Archaeologists. **GLX** agreed to obtain all relevant State of Michigan and/or federal permits required by law for the purposes to conduct limited test excavations of Site 20UM723.

CMURM

Center for Maritime Underwater Resource Management, 2013

What the public was not aware of at the time of this expedition was that we had already discovered the location of the Huron Islands, so this find was important enough to have France's DRASSM team come to assist in identifying the wreck site. We worked diligently to establish a relationship with the Republic of France and the State of Michigan to make this identification. The project required many people giving their time and support and engaging political involvement to accomplish this goal. Finally, with the involvement of State Representative Greg MacMaster, Great Lakes Exploration Group was recognized by the State of Michigan, receiving a Special Tribute from then Governor Rick Snyder, as well as being formally recognized by the Honorable Dan Benishek, M.D. on the floor of the United States House of Representatives. They recognized our work in discovering and preserving the maritime history of the State of Michigan and the Great Lakes through community-based, non-invasive underwater archaeology and research that leaves the bottomlands intact. The State of Michigan recognized that Great Lakes Exploration Group was formed to be a worldwide leader in identifying, protecting, and preserving rare pieces of North American history found in Michigan waters. Figures 1 and 2 are the recognitions by Michigan's governor and politicians.

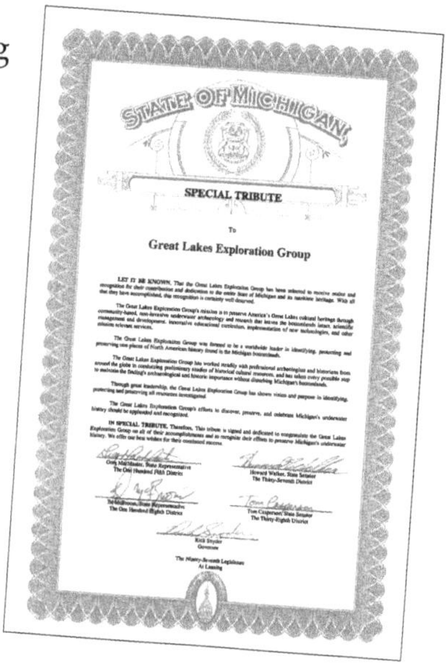

Figure 2
Special Tribute from State of Michigan, 2013

Figure 1

CONGRESSIONAL RECORD:
GREAT LAKES EXPLORATION GROUP

HON. DAN BENISHEK
OF MICHIGAN
IN THE HOUSE OF REPRESENTATIVES

Monday, February 4, 2013
Mr. BENISHEK. Mr. Speaker, I rise today to recognize the Great Lakes Exploration Group on the occasion of the work they do to discover and preserve the maritime history of the State of Michigan and the Great Lakes. The group has not only worked to identify and save historic artifacts, but do so in a way that preserves the cultural heritage of the Great Lakes.

In particular, I wish to commend the Great Lakes Exploration Group on discovering the possible location of Le Griffon, a ship that went missing in 1697. If Le Griffon is found, not only will a centuries-long mystery be solved, but, more importantly, the Great Lakes Group will add to the historical treasure trove of our Nation's earliest days of settlement. Through community-based, *non-invasive Underwater archaeology and research that leaves the bottomlands intact, the Great Lakes Exploration Group was formed to be a worldwide leader in identifying, protecting, and preserving rare pieces of North American history found in Michigan's waters.*

I wish the Great Lakes Exploration Group all the best in locating and preserving the wreck of Le Griffon and learning what secrets it may hold. CONGRESSIONAL RECORD - HON. DAN BENISHEK

The 2013 Expedition – France and Great Lakes Exploration Group

The La Salle–Griffon Project

On June 16, 2013, Great Lakes Exploration Group's international team of American and French archaeologists, along with professional divers, began to excavate site 20UM723 where we had discovered the bowsprit in June of 2001. The friendship project, **The LaSalle–Griffon Project**, received overwhelming public support and inquiries worldwide. It was a magical week, bringing these professionals together for one mission on the Upper Peninsula in a small remote fishing village called Fairport. Fairport is inhabited with the descendants of French and Native Americans. World-renowned scientists from France's DRASSM team, historians, and journalists joined Great Lakes Exploration Group in this historic expedition. Fun-filled events of casual dining, live music, and historical-costumed reenactors entertained the team and spectators.

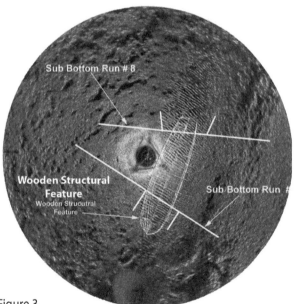

The Expedition became one of the first "live" online media events in underwater archaeological explorations. The national coverage lasted five days. Journalists from *The New York Times,* Fox News, Interlochen Public Radio, and the Associated Press transmitted daily online and radio updates about the expedition. Google search results rated *The New York Time's* article "the number one most viewed online stories for the week."

17th century ship construction expert, Eric Reith, PhD, confirmed in the final French Report that the find was indeed a bowsprit and a very old one. The scientists were expecting to

Figure 3
Sonar showed possible structure buried beneath the bowsprit. White template of ship superimposed. —Abbott Underwater Acoustics

find a ship's hull attached to the structure as the sonar images indicated, but there was no ship to be found (Figure 3). Unknown to the scientists at the time, zebra and quagga mussels skewed the sonar images of the bottom lake bed, rendering false readings of a possible structure buried beneath. Surprisingly, the mussels were over three feet thick in some areas. The technicians determined the shell casings reflected irregular sound acoustics back to the sensor, causing the false readings. Our attempt to identify a ship turned into the recovery of the now famous bowsprit.

The bowsprit and metadata were examined by Michigan's state archaeologist and a scientist from Cornell University at the storage facility. It was at this facility where the bowsprit was completely immersed in a boric acid solution to destroy and prevent harmful fungus and bacteria from growing. A few months after the examination, the state archaeologist would announce the discovery was not that of a bowsprit, but a pound net stake used in the fishing industry to construct traps made of netting and wooden poles. (Figure 4.) They completely disregarded France's expertise in 17th century ship construction, where Eric Reith confirmed the find was a bowsprit. State officials based their conclusion on the similar use of treenails, seldom used in pound net stake construction. They chose to ignore the fact that pound net stakes are pointed on one end, much like that of a pencil. The sharpened end allows the stake to easily penetrate the bottom as they are driven by the use of a pile driver.

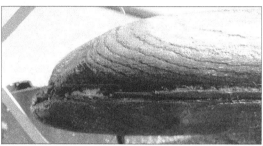

Figure 4
Top: Fishing pound net stakes.
Bottom: Beveled end of bowsprit.

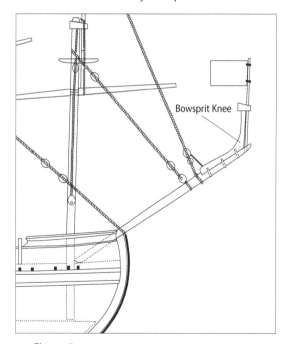

Bowsprit Knee

Figure 5
The measurements of the bowsprit discovered in 2001 is consistent for the size of the ship found in 2018. (Illustration by Kathie Libert)

DRASSM's team of archaeologists, Michel L' Hour, Eric Reith and Olivia Hulot.

The bowsprit has a beveled end, oriented towards the face opposite the scarf face.

The bowsprit's knee would have been mounted on top of the scarf (Figure 5). This orientation is identical to the method used in 17th century French bowsprit construction. It was noted by the French archaeologists in the *Advisory Council on Underwater Archaeology Proceedings 2014* (ACUA) that no other piece of a ship's rigging other than the bowsprit, would have had a scarf at one end and a bevel at the other. More of their comments from this report can be read in Figure 8.

During the excavation of the bowsprit, a hydro lift (dredging equipment) was used to extract the timber, creating a large hole that allowed a diver to descend. It was our hope that the bowsprit was attached to a ship as the preliminary scientific reports depicted. Unfortunately, this was not the case. At the base of the bowsprit, we found two small, unique rectangular pieces of wood (Figures 6 and 7). One of the pieces had a very noticeable carved

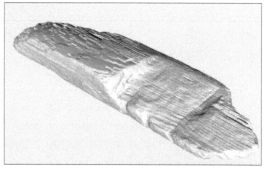

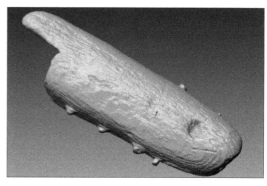

Figures 6 and 7
Imaged from a Handheld Leica Absolute Scanner, these two items were excavated from the base of the recovered bowsprit. Below is one of the actual pieces before the scan.

out impression. This impression was contoured to fit perfectly over the bottom curvature of the bowsprit. We would later identify the two wooden pieces as wedge blocks to secure one end of the bowsprit to its mast step. A pound net stake would have no need for these wedges. This gave us another line of evidence in confirming the timber was a bowsprit. Bowsprits on smaller 17th century French sailing vessels were wedged and not bolted or nailed to secure in place. The main reason being that these spars

Back side of the bowsprit. The top split downward from the large hole that would have connected to the knee holding the flagstaff.

would often break due to the tremendous stress put on the ship's rigging. The bowsprits needed to be quickly and easily replaced.

During the 2013 summer excavation of the bowsprit, French archaeologists and divers Michel L'Hour, Olivia Hulot, and Eric Reith made some provisional conclusions from their observations. These observations were made while the artifact was still underwater (Figure 14, page 43) and before it was completely wrapped in a water-permeable fabric to assist in slowing down the decaying process once at the surface. The French archaeologists would not have the opportunity to thoroughly examine the bowsprit once on land, as the entire structure would be rushed off in a refrigerated truck to a climate-controlled storage facility. It would be months later before any archaeologist or scientist would again examine the bowsprit.

The following excerpt from the *Advisory Council on Underwater Archaeology Proceedings 2014* (ACUA) written by the French archaeologists, gives their conclusions on the structure of the bowsprit.

Figure 8

ACUA REPORT

1. The scarf at the upper end and the bevel at the lower end of the artifact are indeed characteristic of bowsprits.

2. The length of the artifact (6.06 m) is coherent with a bowsprit of a ship of the Griffon's size.

3. The design characteristic of scarfing a knee to the bowsprit to serve as a support for a small mast (for a flag or a sprit topsail) was widely used in the 17th century; however, in France, fell into disuse in the first half of the 18th century.

4. The presence of an erosion ring indicates that the lower part of the artifact, a section measuring 2.62 m in length, had been buried in the sediment of the lake for a long time, at least one hundred years and perhaps even several hundred years.

They went on to note that:

"These conclusions are based on morphological and archaeological observations. They raise new questions to be considered in relation with the latest radiocarbon dating results (Griggs and Vrana 2014)."

The new questions raised in the ACUA Proceedings 2014 referred to the latest radiocarbon dating results that state officials retrieved, using a technique called wiggle-match dating (WMD). The process of C-14 wiggle-matching can be used when it is not possible to date wood samples using dendrochronology (tree ring dating). It requires obtaining multiple radiocarbon measurements taken separately on the subject you want to date, then calibrating them all together to get a set of date ranges. Like separate C-14 tests, the wiggle-matching results usually come back with two to three date range possibilities of when the timber was felled or cut. Archaeologists will then select the best date range based on other known factors of their project, otherwise known as **lines of evidence.** The wiggle match produced a range of the earliest felling and crafting date range of 1700 to 1785 (21.6% probability) and 1820 to 1950 (73.8% probability). In our case, the officials picked the range that best suited them to disclose their belief the timber was a pound net stake. We would select the date range that fits our belief of a bowsprit based on our research, the location of the find, and the French Report. Plus, the historical fact that pound net stakes were not used in this area until 1856. The 1820 to

> **Pound Net Fishing**
>
> The beginning of commercial fishing in Lake Michigan was during the early 1840s at which time haul seine nets were used. By 1846 the industry was utilizing gill nets. During the 1856 time period "pound nets" appeared.
>
> While certainly there are many more types of fishing methods, our primary focus was on the introduction of "pound net" fishing for timeline purposes.

1950 dates offer a wide range and is not substantial evidence in our view, therefore we continue to use the C-14 dates as supporting our theory. The 1700 to 1785 range is twenty-one years off from 1679. This discrepancy could easily be the result of the preservation process of the timber. The timber sat in a bath of boric acid, and if not cleaned properly, could have skewed their results.

The chart below provides the C-14 test results on the bowsprit.

1st Carbon 14–09/30/2003:	1660 to 1950 (95% probability)
2nd Carbon 14–09/12/2013:	1700 to 1720 (95% probability)
3rd Carbon 14–09/23/2013:	1680 to 1740 (95% probability)
09/23/2013:	1680 to 1740 (95% probability)

Note: Test 3 was performed twice as a repeatability check

| 4th Wiggle Match: | 1700 to 1785 (21.6% probability) |
| | 1820 to 1950 (73.8% probability) |

These dates are fitted to a calibration curve, known as curve fitting, built from known-age wood. The curve has a radiocarbon in years scale on the y-axis (vertical line) and calendar years on the x-axis (horizontal line).

These carbon-14 dating analyses were conducted by leading prominent laboratories. All four independent C-14 tests do support the time frame of the building of *Le Griffon* and our hypotheses that the bowsprit could very well be from a ship the age of *Le Griffon*. In our own research to understand this tool, the company's president provided us with enough confirmation to move forward on the bowsprit theory (excerpt below).

> *I am a founding employee and President of Beta Analytic Inc., a company used by archaeologists and geologists worldwide since 1979 for their radiocarbon dating needs. I am a recognized authority in radiocarbon dating, have appeared numerous times on the Discovery Channel, History Channel and BBC and am called upon daily for the measurement, calculation and reporting of radiocarbon dating results to active researchers around the globe.*
>
> *So if I am asked, could this wood be from this ship, the Griffon, downed in AD 1679? The radiocarbon dating results on these two samples do support that time period. However, they also support an age all the way to AD 1950. So the results are not in any way definitive. They must be used as one line of evidence along with others to hopefully provide you with a solution.*

The official announcement from state officials declaring our discovery was nothing more than a pound net stake was very disappointing. We decided to conduct our own thorough examination of the bowsprit and immediately noticed mysterious markings and symbols on the timber. One mark clearly appeared to resemble a stamped uppercase letter "D" with a serif. It was located on the scarf face on the upper portion of the bowsprit (Figure 9). We found it inconceivable that the state archaeologist and a prominent scientist from Cornell overlooked these important features. There was also a faint carving of a winged-like creature on the lower portion. I noticed scribe marks indicating the location as to where treenail holes were to be drilled or positioned (Figure 10 and 11). When constructing ships, carpenters would mark the timbers for many reasons, using Roman numerals, letters, and scribe marks. It is known that sawyers were paid by the footage of timber they produced. We wondered if the letter "D" represented that sawyer's mark for accounting purposes, after all this piece of timber was clearly fashioned for a purpose. The "D" could also represent the French word "derriere," meaning to a position further back or behind. An almost identical inscribed or stamped "D" containing a serif on the lower left portion of the "D" was found on another of La Salle's vessels, *La Belle*. *La Belle* sank in present-day Matagorda Bay off the Texas coast in 1686, seven years after the disappearance of *Le Griffon*. Her wreckage was discovered in 1995 by archaeologists from Texas A&M. The ship was fully excavated in 1996–1997. Perhaps the "D" was graffiti put there by one of the carpenters or crew? At this point we definitely knew that this was not a pound net stake.

Letter "D" found on La Belle. (Photo courtesy of the Texas Historical Commission.)

Figure 9
Letter "D" found on the bowsprit.

Figure 10
Scribe marking treenail location.

The disappointing lack of support from the state prompted us to conduct further research on the bowsprit utilizing newer technology. Scientists from Hexagon Manufacturing Intelligence of Wixom, Michigan, and engineering students from Ferris State University in Big Rapids, Michigan, performed a 3-D scan as a class project using a Leica Absolute Scanner. The handheld scanner provided a digital 3-D model of the bowsprit for analysis. The finished product was extremely impressive (Figure 12).

We were also elated when Gaylord's Otsego Memorial Hospital permitted us to CT scan the bowsprit in hopes of dating tree rings through a science called dendrochronology. Archaeologists have been using MRI technology as a tool for dating artifacts and research for many years. The technology allowed us to view the inside of the timber. Without compromising the structure of the bowsprit, we were able to examine the number of tree rings for dating. Unfortunately, there were an insufficient number of tree rings to determine its date with any accuracy.

In summary, the 2013 Expedition was a successful event in that it solidified relationships and friendships between Great Lakes Exploration Group and France's DRASSM team. The project sent a good-will message internationally and throughout classrooms, reconnecting American history to early French explorers.

The expedition was also a major disappointment. It was not how we

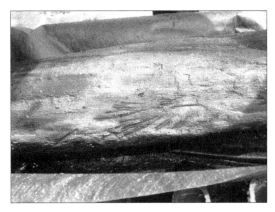

Figure 11
Carving of a wing icon on the bowsprit.

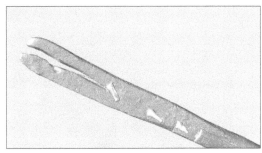

Figure 12
Imaged section of the bowsprit scarf showing treenails from a handheld Leica Absolute Scanner.

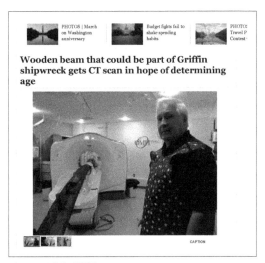

August 24, 2013
Otsego Memorial Hospital.

anticipated the conclusion of the project but I vividly recalled Michel L'Hour quietly saying to me that he believed the ship is within 4 miles of the bowsprit. That is what experience gives you. So, the search continued. In the summer of 2018, within 3.8 miles of the bowsprit, we discovered a very old ship of colonial-age that we believe could possibly be Robert La Salle's long-lost vessel, *Le Griffon*.

Media

May 28, 2006
Le Journal du Dimanche.

The Letter "D"

The marking of the "D" brings up more questions. La Salle's ship, *La Belle*, was discovered in Matagorda Bay, Texas, in 1995 with identical markings of the letter "D" on its timbers. *La Belle* was built in France in 1684. The "D" appears to be carved or stamped in both instances, with approximately similar dimensions of 20mm x 20mm (Figure 9). It is now known that *La Belle* used master frames, and was supposedly built as a kit. The "D" brings up the possibility of whether Moïse Hillaret, La Salle's shipwright, used master frames for building *Le Griffon*. If so, the master frames could have been measured and cut in Montreal at the King's shipyard, then sent up river to be carried over the falls to the makeshift shipyard on Cayuga Creek. Hillaret would have used these key master frames to determine the lines of the boat and finish the completion of the hull.

Infrared image of bowsprit (2001).

Ownership of *Le Griffon* — *Admiralty Law/Foreign Sovereign Immunities Act*

The litigation between Great Lakes Exploration Group LLC., trigraph **(GLX),** and the State of Michigan resulted in **GLX** wanting to protect our salvage rights to *Le Griffon* versus the State of Michigan's attempt to divest the federal court of jurisdiction and laying an ownership claim to *Le Griffon*.

Contrary to the claims of many state government officials, states do not own everything on their bottomlands, especially when it pertains to shipwrecks.

For a state to legally claim ownership, the shipwreck must be **both** abandoned and embedded on their bottomlands.

All cases of admiralty and maritime matters fall under the judicial powers of the United States Government, as per Article III, § 2 of the U.S. Constitution.

> **Section 2.**
>
> The judicial power shall extend to all cases, in law and equity, arising under this Constitution, the laws of the United States, and treaties made, or which shall be made, under their authority; — to all cases affecting ambassadors, other public ministers and consuls; — **to all cases of admiralty and maritime jurisdiction**; — to controversies to which the United States shall be a party; — to controversies between two or more states; — between a state and citizens of another state; — between citizens of different states; — between citizens of the same state claiming lands under grants of different states, and between a state, or the citizens thereof, and foreign states, citizens or subjects.
>
> The U.S. Code Title 43. Public Lands Chapter 39. Abandoned Shipwreck distinguishes which shipwrecks are subject to ownership of a State.
>
> **(b)**
>
> included in the range of resources are **certain** abandoned shipwrecks, which have been deserted and to which the owner has relinquished ownership rights with no retention.

The statute above clearly states that only certain shipwrecks fall into the ownership of a state. The law of salvage and the law of finds are often very complicated legal issues. Today, most legal claims to long-lost vessels come under the umbrella of the Abandoned Shipwreck Act, passed into law in 1988. In the case of *Le Griffon,* the ASA of 1988 did not apply. However, the Foreign Sovereign Immunities Act of 1976 would have been at issue had the case proceeded further and before an admirable agreement was reached with Great Lakes Exploration Group, France, and Michigan.

"The property of a sovereign is not abandoned unless the sovereign expressly renounces title. France has not renounced title to Le Griffon.*"*

—Rick Robol, Attorney for Great Lakes Exploration Group in a March 28, 2009 filing. (*Detroit AP/ Traverse City Record-Eagle* April 9, 2009)

CONSERVATION OF BOWSPRIT

To help conserve the artifact, while it was underwater, archaeologists completely wrapped the bowsprit in a water-permeable fabric. The timber was then put into a makeshift cradle to prevent damage while being raised from the bottom of the lake. Once on the surface, the timber needed to be protected from the sun's destructive ultraviolet rays. The fabric was kept watered down and the bowsprit stored in a refrigerated truck where it was quickly transported to a climate-controlled storage facility. While at the facility, it was immersed in a boric acid solution bath to destroy and prevent harmful fungus and bacteria from reoccurring.

The following Letters of Patent (Figure 13) is the actual document that the Republic of France used to claim *Le Griffon* as a sovereign ship in 2013. The document was submitted to federal court in response to the State of Michigan's claim to the ship. During Great Lakes Exploration Group's 2013 Expedition, some of the public misunderstood France's involvement and thought the French were trying to interfere and make claim to a ship they did not have legal rights to. In fact, without their participation the 2013 Expedition would not have taken place. We requested France's involvement. The Letters of Patent solidified France's ownership, persuading the State of Michigan to grant Great Lakes Exploration Group a limited permit. Michigan would not accept our request without France's participation.

We are very grateful for the DRASSM team led by divers Michel L'Hour, Olivia Hulot, and Dr. Eric Reith (France's Department of Underwater and Submarine Archaeological Research). France's archaeologists are some of the most elite professionals in the world, and Dr. Eric Reith's knowledge of 17th century shipbuilding brought a wealth of information to the team. We were honored when they accepted the invitation to participate in the 2013 Expedition.

Figure 13

Letters of Patent

Granted by the King of France to the Sieur de La Salle, on the 12th of May, 1678

Translation

Louis, by the grace of God, King of France and of Navarre. To our dear and well-loved Robert Cavelier, Sieur de la Salle, greeting:

We have received with favor the very humble petition, which has been presented to us in your name, to permit you to endeavor to discover the western part of New France; and we have consented to this proposal the more willingly, because there is nothing we have more at heart than the discovery of this country, through which it is probable a road may be found to penetrate to Mexico [dans laquel il y a apprarence que l'on trouvera un chemin pour penetrar justqu'au Mexique]; and because your diligence in clearing the lands which we granted to you by the decree of our council of the 13th of May, 1675, and, by Letters of Patent of the same date, to form habitations upon the said lands, and to put Fort Frontenac in a good state of defense, the seigniory and government whereof we likewise granted to you, affords us every reason to hope that you will succeed to our satisfaction, and to advantage of our subjects of the said country.

For these reasons, and others thereunto moving us, we have permitted, and do hereby permit you, by these presents, signed by our hand, to endeavor to discover the western part of New France, and, for the execution of this enterprise, to construct forts wherever you shall deem it necessary; which it is our will that you shall hold on the same terms and conditions as Fort Frontenac, agreeably and conformably to our said Letters Patent of 13th of March, 1675, which we have confirmed, as far as is needful, and hereby confirm by these presents. And it is our pleasure that they be executed according to their form and tenor.

To accomplish this, and everything above mentioned, we give you full powers; on condition, however, that you shall finish this enterprise within five years, in default of which these presents shall be void and of none effect; that you carry on no trade whatever with the savages called Outaouacs, and others who bring their beaver skins and other peltries to Montreal; and that the whole shall be done at your expense, and that of your company, to which we have granted the privilege of the trade in buffalo skins. And we command the Sieur de Frontenac, our Governor and Lieutenant-General, and the Sieur Duchense, Intendant, and the other officers who compose the supreme council of the said country, to affix their signatures to these presents; for such is our pleasure. Given at St Germain en Laye, this 12th day of May, 1678, and of our reign the thirty-fifth.

[Signed]
Louis.
And lower down, By the King,
Colbert

And sealed with the great seal with yellow wax.
The act of the Governor, attached to these presents, is
Dated the 5th of November, 1678.

The La Salle – Griffon Project 2013 Expedition
Photos of Discovery

Great Lakes Diving and Salvage provided a team of commercial divers who helped archaeologists excavate the area.

Photographer: David Ruck

Great Lakes Exploration Group's diver checks out the bowsprit before test excavation.

Photographer: David Ruck

DRASSM archaeologist Olivia Hulot adjusts her buoyancy to descend to the wreck site.

Photographer: David Ruck

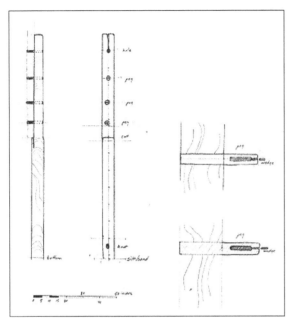

Figure 14

Eric Reith's preliminary illustration of the bowsprit. Reith holds a PhD in Ship Archaeology and Technical History.

A Blessing given by Tribal Chairperson Aaron Payment of the Sault Tribe of Chippewa Indians.

Reid Louis reenacts La Salle and sings "Alouette" with the Voyagers.

*The Voyagers arrive in handcrafted canoes on a Fairport, Michigan, beach as **GLX** team and guests look on.*

La Salle lands his canoe with three Voyagers.

*Historical records tell us
the location of the
Huron Islands and offer clues
to where Le Griffon met her fate.*

Chapter 4

The Huron Islands

Discovery Through Maps

When searching for the wreckage of *Le Griffon*, locating the true Huron Islands was the most important piece of the puzzle. For some locals, these islands were known through local folklore songs, or having knowledge of the Native American history surrounding the Upper Peninsula of Michigan and Door County, Wisconsin. We had heard one of these folk songs in 1981, the lyrics telling of the 1653 Iroquois War, the Huron Indians, and Huron Island. Hundreds of men, children, and elders were killed during this war. The lyrics connected Huron Island to present day Washington Island in Green Bay, Wisconsin. We had wondered then, if this was the chain of islands where *Le Griffon* disappeared. The Iroquois War was such a traumatic event that it would take over fifteen years before these islands were inhabited again, but not by Hurons. The Potawatomie people were there when La Salle visited.

Le Griffon ended her maiden voyage among these beautiful islands. The confusion as to where these islands were located in present time added to the mystery of the legend. Some historians believed they were in Lake Huron, others in the Beaver Island chain in Lake Michigan. We will show you that these mysterious islands are in Lake Michigan, protecting the entrance to Green Bay. They include Washington Island, Rock Island, St. Martin Island, Gull Islands, Poverty Island, Big Summer Island, and Little Summer Island. The French referred to these islands as the Huron Islands, as noted in primary source documents. Kathie and I will take you through our journey of discovery and provide a little history on the Huron Islands, supported with 17th century maps. We will also divulge the CLUES used to locate and confirm these islands through historical documents. Our research tells the story and produces the facts that the Huron Islands are in northern Lake Michigan.

In 1983, while researching the archives in the Detroit Public Library, I uncovered information that led me to the discovery of where *Le Griffon* met her fate. It was a momentous, historic moment for me. Throughout the years, Kathie and I would continue to gather information from primary source documents and 17th century maps and charts. Then, in 2001, convinced we were among *Le Griffon's* Huron Islands and with the discovery of what appeared to be a bowsprit, we began our quest to confirm the wreck site. We formed the Great Lakes Exploration Group (**GLX**) and initiated **The La Salle–Griffon Project** in 2003 in order to identify the timber and locate the wreck among these elusive Islands.

The Huron Indians and the Iroquois War — Discovery Through Maps

Washington Island had been referred to as Huron Island by Jesuit explorers as early as 1670. The Huron Indians inhabited these islands, establishing a village on the largest of them, Huron Island, present day Washington Island. Green Bay was mapped as the Baye of Puans. Today, these islands form the entrance to Green Bay and are often referred to as the Garden Islands, getting their name from the Garden Peninsula of Michigan.

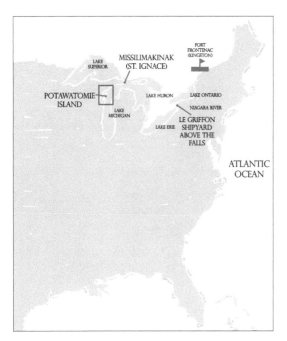 

The Huron Islands are in Lake Michigan. The largest island, called Potawatomie Island, is present-day Washington Island, also once called Huron Island. The chain of islands extend northward to the Garden Peninsula. These islands include Washington Island, Rock Island, St. Martin Island, Gull Islands, Poverty Island, Big Summer Island, and Little Summer Island.

In 1653, the Iroquois War devastated many of the native Indians living around the Great Lakes, including the Huron and the Ottawa. Hundreds were killed when the Iroquois sent a war party of eight hundred men to attack Huron Island (Washington Island). The Hurons and Ottawas hastily abandoned the island and fled to the Potawatomie who were encamped on the southwest shores of Green Bay (Baye Des Puans). By 1655, the Iroquois had swept the islands around Lake Michigan clean of all inhabitants. The Huron's disastrous defeat by the Iroquois in 1653 had them fleeing all directions, including east and south of Georgian Bay in Lake Huron. From 1655 to 1670, there was no safe haven for them east of Wisconsin, except in the vicinity of the French settlements.

The 1675 map in Figure 15 is accredited to La Salle's agent Abbé Claude Bernou in Paris. It is a significant find and shows us the location of these islands. The map includes four islands at the mouth of Green Bay in Lake Michigan, along with a note in French,

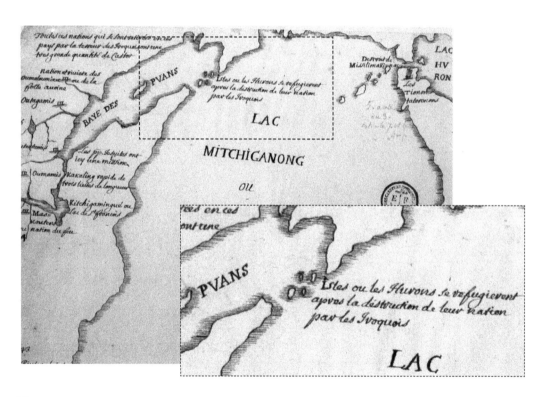

Figure 15

This 1675 map from the "Research Laboratories of Archaeology" is credited to La Salle's Paris agent, Claude Bernou. It shows where the Huron Islands are located in Lake Michigan, and clearly distinguishes them from the Beaver Island chain. The map depicts the Huron Islands between Wisconsin's Door County Peninsula and Michigan's Garden Peninsula. The translation reads "Islands where the Hurons took refuge after the destruction of their nation by the Iroquois."

that when translated reads: *Islands where the Hurons took refuge after the destruction of their nation by the Iroquois.* The location of Huron Island is also supported through historical documents by historians, early explorers, and Jesuits who traversed the area around Wisconsin and Green Bay. They are as follows:

> *Nicolas Perrot in his* Memoir on the Manners, Customs, and Religion of the Savages of North America, *gives an account of this settlement and calls the place Huron Island.*

> *Peter Espirit Raddison's account in* The Jesuit Relations and Voyages — an Account of His Travels and Experiences among the North American Indians, from 1652 to 1684, *gives the island the same name.*

> *Historian Francis Parkman's* The Jesuits in North America in the Seventeenth Century, *translates many of the French documents in 1867 and also places the Huron's living there on the island which is now Washington Island.*

In 1671, the Potawatomie would eventually establish a village on Huron Island (Washington Island), and were described by the French to be very warlike and hostile to the Iroquois, frequently inflicting severe blows on them. It's no wonder, considering their past with the Iroquois. La Potherie, a French historian, describes these Indians in his *Histoire de l'Amerique septentrionale* (1640–1660) as very intelligent, sensible, deliberate, and seldom undertaking any unreasonable enterprise.

NATIVE AMERICAN TIMELINE IN THE DOOR COUNTY REGION FOR 1634–1687

1634	*Winnebagos*	**Other Notable Indian Tribes in Region**
1641	*Potawatomis*	*Menominees*
1651	*Wyandot and Ottawa moved to Huron Island in Green Bay, merged with Potawatomis*	*Noquet*
		Ojibwe
1653	*Potawatomis*	*Odawa*
1658	*Wyandot leaves Island area*	*Fox*
1665	*Ottawa and Hurons return*	
1667	*Sauk/Sac*	
		Hostile Tribes
		Iroquois
1670-1672	*Wyandot (Hurons)*	*Dakota*
1665-1687	*Potawatomi remained in the region*	*Mohawk*
		Seneca

Figure 16
The 1688 map, "Partie occidentale du Canada ou de la Nouvelle," shows the Village of the Potawatomie on Huron Island and an Indian hunting encampment on either Big Summer or Poverty Island.

A close-up picture of the 1688 *Partie occidentale du Canada ou de la Nouvelle* map of New France in Figure 16 shows the Potawatomie Village on Huron Island and an Indian hunting encampment which appears to be on Big Summer or Poverty Island. This encampment and map are important to *Le Griffon's* story, and we reference it again during our description of the barque's disappearance among these islands in Chapter 6, page 73. The map above is a collaboration, using sources from La Salle, Marquette, Joliet, and mapmaker Jean-Baptiste-Louis Franquelin. Franquelin received most of his information directly from French explorers. Further information on this particular map is on page 50. The map was created by Vincenzo Coronelli and Jean Nicolas du Tralage, sieur de Tillemon, and then produced and published in 1688 by publisher Jean Baptiste Nolin. They had gathered these resources and created what is considered one of the best representations of the period of the Great Lakes during this time.

Figure 17 shows a Franquelin (ca. 1650+) map placing the *Les Huronnes* Islands in Lake Michigan, but not drawn at the entrance to Green Bay. They were placed far to the east of the entrance, making some *Griffon* seekers believe they represented the Beaver Island chain. Further research shows that the information Franquelin received when drawing

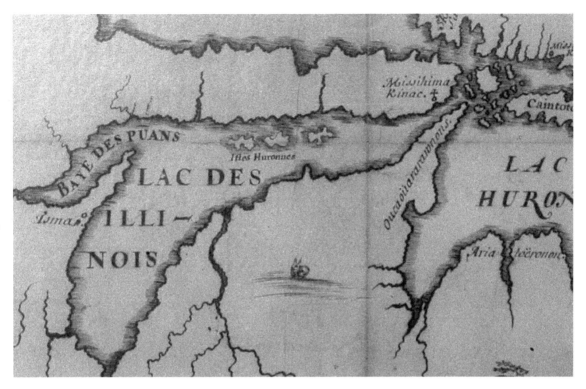

Figure 17
Jean-Baptiste-Louis Franquelin (ca. 1650–17). This earlier map shows the Les Huronnes Islands but are drawn far east of the entrance to the Baye of Puans (Green Bay).

this map focused on the northern coast, the same coastline *Le Griffon* would have followed. They had not begun to explore the Beaver Island chain at this time, giving a false sense of where the Huron Islands were located.

The mystery surrounding the location of the Huron Islands, and where *Le Griffon* met her fate, created a larger-than-life legend. It initiated a search by adventurers and historians that would include all of the upper Great Lakes. Some contemporary historians put the Huron Islands in Lake Huron. After the Iroquois War, many of the Huron and Ottawa Indians went east and settled on islands in Lake Huron to be close to French settlements for safety. When French explorer Peter Radisson returned to Montreal from his voyage southwest of Lake Michigan (which began on August 6, 1654, and ended late in August, 1656), he was in the thick of the Iroquois War. He had asked for the assistance of the Tobacco Hurons to come home to Montreal with him and his men. He knew his trip would be dangerous and had decided to ask for their assistance.

These Hurons were familiar with the military tactics of the Iroquois and could be depended upon to withstand a determined attack, which in fact did happen. Radisson credits the Hurons for their survival.

The Hurons, who accompanied Radisson during his expedition back home, found their wives and children on Bois Blanc in the northern part of Lake Huron and south of Georgian Bay. Many of the Ottawas and Hurons had scattered there and would make Michilimackinac, the region around the Straits of Mackinac and Mackinac Island, a permanent home. They eventually moved to St. Ignace Mission in 1671. Nowhere is there any reference in historical documents to calling Michilimackinac, or the islands among Georgian Bay area, *Le Griffon's* famed Huron Islands.

Partie occidentale du Canada ou de la Nouvelle

www.americanjourneys.org — see map on page 51

Accession Number	*36187*
File Name	*36187-19*
Call number	*Cabinet OVERSIZE Cartographie du Canada*
Map title	*Partie occidentale du Canada ou de la Nouvelle France ou sont les Nations des Ilinois, de Tracy, les Iroquois, et plusieurs autres Peuples ...*
Place of Publication	*Paris*
Publisher	*Chez J. B. Nolin [Jean Baptiste Nolin] ...*
Publication date	*1688*
Map size height	*44.4 cm.*
Map size width	*59.5 cm.*
Item description	*engraving, hand coloring*

Geographical description: *Map of New France, including the Great Lakes and the area around the Mississippi River.*

Cartobibliographic notes: *This map is a collaboration between Coronelli, Tillemon, and Nolin. It is one of the best representations of the period of the Great Lakes, particularly Lake Superior. Sources for the information shown on the map include Marquette, Joliet, and La Salle. Jean Baptiste-Louis Franquelin, who was based in Quebec and received much of the information brought by the French explorers, was also a significant source of information for this map. This map was number 19 in a made-up atlas, Cartographie du Canada, assembled by Henry Harrisse and later bought by Samuel Latham Brown. It was disbound when purchased and is held separately by the Library.*

References: *Burden, P.D. Mapping of North America, II, 630; Kaufman, K. The Mapping of the Great Lakes in the Seventeenth Century, no. 12; www.pequotmuseum.org/uploaded_images/CC2DB15E-FC71-4988-BC3D-4481CE-33CA70/CartoIInew.pdf (Oct. 2007)*

Geographic Area	*North America*
Normalized date	*1688*
Creator	*Vincenzo Coronelli*
Creator	*Jean Nicolas du Tralage, sieur de Tillemon*

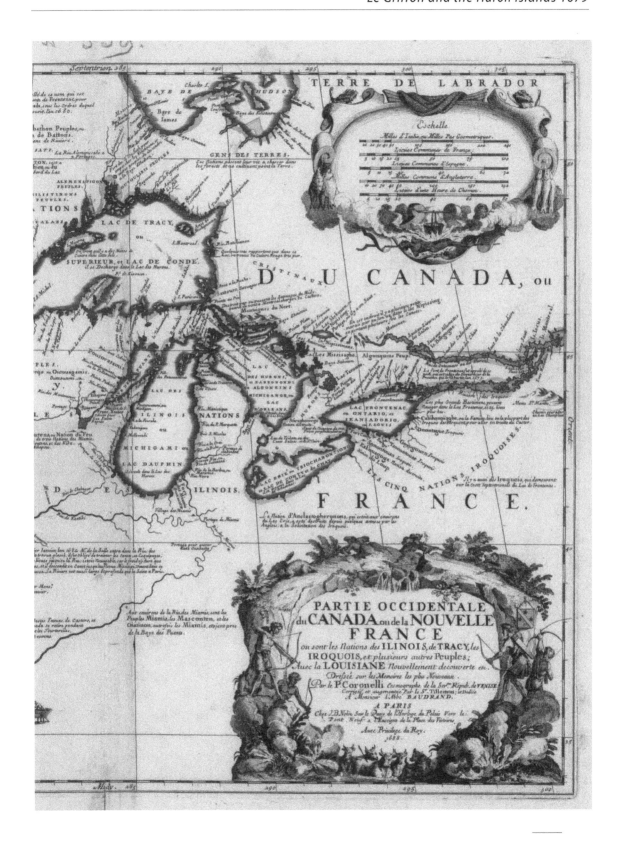

LaSalle – Griffon Project
IDENTIFICATION TEAM

Chapter 5

In Search of *Le Griffon* Among the Huron Islands

Through Primary Source Documents and Exploration

As we mentioned earlier, the main piece of the puzzle in searching for *Le Griffon's* resting place was discovering the **location** of the Huron Islands. The three main documents that provide the most information of *Le Griffon's* maiden voyage and demise around these islands comes from La Salle's letters to his agent Abbé Claude Bernou in Paris, who documented La Salle's activities from 1679 to 1681 in *Relation of Discoveries (1682).* The second document provides a "path measure," which we refer to as a navigational course, from Claude-Charles La Potherie, a historian born in Paris in

Aerial view of the Huron Islands from Fairport, MI.
Photo by Eagle Eye Drone Service, Kewadin, Michigan

1663. His work, titled *Histoire de l'Amerique Septentrionale,* or *History of Northern America,* was submitted for publication in 1702, but was not published until 14 years later. The last document comes from Father Louis Hennepin, who accompanied La Salle on his voyage. While Hennepin cannot be considered absolutely reliable because of his known plagiarizing and embellishments, he was the scribe on the expedition. He provides us with an eyewitness account from Niagara to Lake Michigan while he sailed and made notes from the deck of *Le Griffon.* Hennepin's 1698 *New Discovery of a Vast Country in America* provides detailed information that fills important gaps. We believe his notes from this voyage to be credible for our research. We were able to deduce important descriptions from Hennepin's writings and with my knowledge and 40-year experience in the area. Hennepin's voyage notes were made early enough in the expedition for us to conclude that he had penned some important moments, some while La Salle was probably not even present.

There were many contemporary sources early on that inspired our research, including *Indian Culture and European Trade Goods* by George Irving Quimby (1966). Quimby referenced historian La Potherie, who gave specific navigational distances to *Le Griffon's* journey, leading us to research his primary source documents. Between La Salle, La Potherie, and Father Hennepin's accounts, along with my *own* experiences among those islands, we had gathered enough information to convince us where the Huron Islands were, and thus the probable wreck site of *Le Griffon*. Unfortunately for La Salle, Hennepin was known for plagiarizing, and their documents are quite similar in many ways. They do give us some insight into the times and difficulties La Salle faced during his expeditions, as well as what happened after his death, when Hennepin tried to claim he had secretly discovered the mouth of the Mississippi before La Salle.

Our research here and quest to find *Le Griffon's* resting place focuses on excerpts from those three main primary source documents of La Salle, La Potherie, and Hennepin. In managing these documents, we layered them like transparencies on top of each other. Once this was completed, we could see a story emerge, a living document that will continue to expand as the ship is excavated and more stories are added. Our knowledge of early history is ever-expanding, and by eliminating the unnecessary "static" (parts that are less important to our research) we were able to focus and accomplish our goals.

In Search of *Le Griffon's* Location

The search for *Le Griffon's* resting place among the Huron Islands is not only based on our research, but my previously mentioned knowledge and experience of over 40 years diving around these islands. The bowsprit recovered during the 2013 Expedition was in the correct geographical area described in the historical documents of *Le Griffon's* final last moments. We also believed that the hull of this ship would be found within four miles. The following excerpts from these documents highly supported our conclusion that this historical ship is among Poverty Island, Big Summer, and Little Summer Island. We were convinced the ship was in the area, but we also knew that finding the wreck site was going to take some time.

The following pages reveal 8-CLUES we derived from these documents in search of *Le Griffon*. The La Salle, La Potherie, and Hennepin manuscripts provided the information we needed to uncover the location of the Huron Islands and *Le Griffon's* final resting place.

1–5 CLUES FROM LA SALLE

Le Griffon **Disappears — La Salle's Story**

The first primary source document originates from La Salle's own account, where he describes *Le Griffon*'s final moments before the ship disappeared from sight. He also confirms the location of the Huron Islands in the second excerpt, page 55. The first excerpt below is from La Salle's letter sent to his agent Abbé Claude Bernou in Paris on September 29, 1680, a year after he lost his ship. La Salle gives us the first clue — the wind was westerly, favorable for going to Missilimakinak. La Salle's account learned from the Potawatomie Indians implies that his ship never made it out of the chain of islands from where it left anchor at Washington Island. He states that the ship headed *"obliquely towards some islands in the offing blocked by great sand banks, which extend outwards more than two leagues."* Here we have bolded the clues in the excerpts used for discovery — the facts that put the puzzle together, quoted again:

> Some Indians, called Pouteatamis, tell me that two days after the vessel left the island where I had quitted here on the 18th of September 1679, this storm arose, of which I have told you: and the pilot, who had anchored with them on the northern coast, where they were encamped, **believing the wind to be favorable for going to Missilimakinak, as in fact it was out in the lake, set sail contrary to their advice, not perceiving the violence of the wind because the land over which it blew was so near.** They assured him that there was a great tempest in the offing, where the lake seemed all white: but the pilot laughed at them, replying that his vessel was not afraid of the wind, and set sail. The wind increased very much, and they observed that he was obliged to furl all his sails except two large ones: and after that, **the barque could not keep a straight course, but drove obliquely towards some islands in the offing blocked by great sand banks, which extend outwards more than two leagues.** Then the wind became still more violent, with very heavy rain and they lost sight of the vessel. Nothing was heard of it until the spring, when two pairs of linen breeches, spoiled with pitch and all torn, were found on the coast: and finally, this summer, they found a hatchway, a bit of cordage and some packets of beaver-skin, all spoiled. All this made them believe that the barque had run aground somewhere on these islands, and was lost with all that was in it.

Not only does La Salle's account imply that *Le Griffon* never made it out of this chain of islands after it left anchor at Washington Island, his description of the sandbanks extending more than two leagues is quite telling. The only area that fits this description in northern Lake Michigan are within this chain of islands that stretches across the entrance to Green Bay, Wisconsin, to the Garden Peninsula. Again, these islands include Washington Island, Rock Island, St. Martin Island, Gull Islands, Poverty Island, Big Summer Island, and Little Summer Island. The sandbar runs from a northwest to a southeast direction between Little Summer and Big Summer Island. (See satellite image on page 64, Figure 18.) The question was: Are these the Huron Islands? The map in Figure 15, page 46, from Claude Bernou tells us they are.

Huron Islands in Lake of the Illinois (Lake Michigan)

The next clue comes from the following description from one of La Salle's letters dated November 11, 1680, to his agent Abbé Claude Bernou. Bernou gives a quick summary of La Salle's trip into the Illinois Country to build Fort Crevecoeur, present day Creve Coeur, a suburb of Peoria, overlooking the Illinois River. The information from La Salle confirms the location and the name of the islands through Bernou's summary:

> *The Sieur de La Salle arrived in Canada on the 15th of September 1678 with authority to explore the countries to which the great river called the Mississippi leads. He wintered at Fort Frontenac, where he had a barque built at a place called Niagara; he afterwards embarked with twenty-two men, to cross Lake Erie, and entered the Lake of the Hurons: he then came and anchored at a place called Missilimakinac, which is the great meeting place of the Outaouas tribes.*
>
> *From that place **he advanced on the <u>Lake of the Illinois</u> as far as <u>the Huron Islands</u>** and, having sent back his barque, he pushed on from there with eight canoes and came to a village of the Illinois...*
>
> *(Relation of the Discoveries and Voyages of Cavelier de La Salle from 1679 to 1681: The Official Narrative)*

La Salle clearly puts the Huron Islands on the Lake of the Illinois (Lake Michigan)

Le Griffon's first maiden voyage took La Salle to the Huron Islands, specifically present day Washington Island, where he met up with some of his men who were sent there earlier to trap and collect furs from the Potawatomie. Under La Salle's order, the men had traded goods for beaver pelts from the local Indians. Washington Island is one of a string of islands (which are an outcropping of

the Niagara Escarpment) geologically stretching across the entrance of Green Bay from the Door County Peninsula in Wisconsin to the Garden Peninsula in Michigan.

The earliest records and maps of the French, with whom written history of the region begins, do not name the individual islands, but refer to them all as a group. The names chosen depended upon which group of Native Americans inhabited the islands at the time. The most common name after 1650 to 1816 was the Potawatomie Islands. The Jesuit Records of 1670–1672, however, refer to this chain of islands as the Huron Islands (see graphic below). Huron in French also translates into the meaning of boorish or rough. Certainly these terms are fitting in describing the harsh environment surrounding these islands during and after severe weather. Other references for these islands, named after the Ojibwa who once inhabited the area were called the Noquet Islands. Today the bay that opens into Lake Michigan's Green Bay is known as Big Bay de Noc. It is known the Ojibwa once made present day Washington Island their home. American explorer, Jonathan Carver, who traveled the area in the mid-1760s, referred to these islands as "Islands of the Grand Traverse."

Washington Island

On July 1816, Col. John Miller was in charge of garrisoning a new fort at the head of Green Bay called Fort Howard. The three schooners, *Wayne, Mink*, and *Washington*, the largest of the three and one sloop called *Ameila* sailed from Mackinac Island. The fleet was separated en route, and the Washington anchored in what is now Washington Harbor to wait for the others. There they named the harbor after the ship and in honor of President George Washington.

The Jesuit Relations and Allied Documents — Travels and Explorations of the Jesuit Missionaries In New France, 1610 –1791, Vol. LV, 1670–1672:

Relation of the Missions to the Outouacs during the years 1670 and 1671.

"Finally, between this Lake of the Ilinois and Lake Superior is seen a long bay called the Bay des Puans, at the head of which is the Mission of Saint François Xavier; while at its entrance are encountered the islands called Huron, because the Hurons took refuge there for some time, after their own country was laid waste."

(Refer to larger map, page 46.)

Maps and Documents Confirm the Location of the Huron Islands

Until recently, finding 17th century maps was quite difficult. It is understandable why many believed the Huron Islands to be in Lake Huron. Research and primary source documents positively locate these islands. As you have seen in Figure 15, page 46, the map accredited to La Salle's agent Claude Bernou shows *Isels ou les Hurons* next to the islands that lie between Door County, Wisconsin, and the Garden Peninsula in Michigan. **La Salle himself would have given Bernou the information to create the map.** This map clearly shows that *Le Griffon* did not go down around the Beaver Island chain where some have thought. It solidified the geographical area for our search for *Le Griffon.*

Summary of Clues: *La Salle's documents give the first five clues in search of the location for the Huron Islands and the possible location for* Le Griffon.

Clue 1 • La Salle implies that his flagship goes down in the same chain of islands where she had anchored on Washington Island.

Clue 2 • La Salle describes the location having a sandbar that extends more than 2 leagues (1 league equals 2.4 to 3 statute miles).

Clue 3 • La Salle confirms in a letter to his Paris agent that clearly puts the Huron Islands on the Lake of the Illinois — Lake Michigan.

Clue 4 • The 1675 map from La Salle's agent clearly places the Huron Islands between Door County, Wisconsin, and the Garden Peninsula in Michigan.

Clue 5 • The map confirms that *Le Griffon* did not go down among the Beaver Island chain of islands.

Fast approaching northwest storm heading for Poverty Island.

Photo by Steve Libert

6-CLUE FROM LA POTHERIE

La Potherie's Path Measure

A Navigational Course

"X" marks the spot comes from historian Claude-Charles La Potherie's *Histoire de l'Amerique septentrionale* (Blair, 1911, I, 353). He provides us with the sixth clue, a path measure which gave us a detailed navigational route and distance where *Le Griffon's* maiden voyage ended. Using his path measure, we calculated the proximity of where *Le Griffon* anchored and where the ship disappeared. We go into more details later using illustrated charts detailing our navigational thoughts based on the clues provided. La Potherie states that the flagship was driven by a storm into a small bay. His account of this follows and says the ship:

> "…*was driven by a storm **into a small bay, five or six leagues from the anchorage which it had left**,*" *(and boarded by a party of Ottawa Indians who then killed the crew and burned the ship.)*

The text in parentheses is unnecessary "static" at this time and gets in the way of charting a navigational route in search of locating *Le Griffon*. However, the information may be important for other reasons explained later on in this book. *Le Griffon's* disappearance is a mystery and there were several theories of what may have happened. La Salle's own belief was stated in a letter to the Governor of New France, Antoine Lefebvre, Sieur de La Barre on June 4, 1683 (Parkman, 1894, p. 301), four years after *Le Griffon* disappeared. He came to believe his barque was intentionally destroyed by the pilot and crew and eventually captured by Indians. Ultimately the wreckage may tell the final story of *Le Griffon's* crew and final demise.

More importantly is that La Potherie's information gives us a path measure and states that *Le Griffon* sailed **five or six leagues** from Washington Island and anchored in a small bay because of a storm. We charted the sequences from these clues in the next chapter.

La Potherie is like our modern day investigative journalist who focused on investigating and recording historical accounts. His path measure, which I like to refer to it as, indicates that there was obviously an investigation into how and where this ship went down. Both La Salle and Hennepin mention in their documents that a hatch cover, two pairs of britches, the trunk of the flagstaff, spoiled pelts and the door to the cabin were found, indicating La Salle knew the general area of where the ship disappeared. In 1691, La Potherie had held the post of chief writer in the Marine at Brest until 1697. In 1702, La Potherie submitted his manuscript to the royal censor in Paris, who received it favorably, but he had to wait fourteen years to see it published. La Potherie, an historian and writer, was known to be detailed and informative in his writings, and it is easy to accept this information from his own investigation of the disappearance of *Le Griffon*.

Summary of Clue: *La Potherie's documents give a navigational path and the sixth clue that supports the area of the location of the sandbar.*

Clue 6 • La Potherie's Path Measure of five or six leagues led us to our final search area. It directs us northward to the location of the small bay, Indian encampment and sandbar.
(See map on page 68 for more details.)

Drawing of a canoe from La Potherie's document "Histoire de l'Amerique septentrionale."

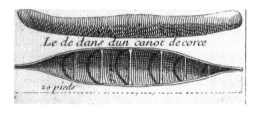

Etching of Quebec Harbor from La Potherie's document "Histoire de l'Amerique septentrionale."

7–8 CLUES FROM LA SALLE & HENNEPIN

La Salle's Account

Buried in the Sand – Confirms *Le Griffon* went Down Among the Huron Islands

La Salle and Hennepin's manuscripts provide us with a geographical description of *Le Griffon's* resting place. Their accounts below deliver the final two clues that confirm the shallow water and that the ship was buried in the sands. La Salle confirms that *Le Griffon* went down among the Huron Islands.

Le Griffon's shipyard etching from Hennepin's *manuscript with an inscribed Griffon on the stern.*

La Salle:

They set sail on the 18th of September, with a light but very favorable west wind. What route they took has never been ascertained; and although there is no doubt they were lost, it has been impossible to learn any circumstances of their shipwreck, except the following.

The vessel having cast anchor in the northern part of Lake Illinois, the pilot, against the advice of some Savages who warned him there was a great storm outside, persisted in setting sail, without considering that the sheltered position of the ship prevented him from perceiving the violence of the wind. **Scarcely was the ship a quarter League from land,** *when the Savages saw it tossing frightfully, unable to make head against the storm, although all the sails had been struck; a short time after, they lost it from sight,* **and think it to have been driven upon shallows near the Huron Islands, where it has been buried in the sand.** *It is not until the following year that M. de La Salle learned all these things. Certain it is that the loss of this vessel cost him more than forty thousand livres, counting not only goods, tools, and peltry, but also the men and rigging which he had brought from France to Canada, and had transported from Montreal to Fort Frontenac in bark canoes, — a feat seeming impossible to those acquainted with the fragility of such craft, considering the weight of anchors and cables.*

(Relation of the Discoveries and Voyages of Cavelier de La Salle from 1679 to 1681: The Official Narrative)

Hennepin's Account

Hennepin's narrative is consistent with La Salle's in confirming the shallow water and that the ship was buried in the sand.

Father Hennepin:

They sailed the 18th of September with a Westerly Wind, and fir'd a Gun to take their leave. Tho' the Wind was favourable, it was never known what Course they steer'd, nor how they perishe'd; for after all the Enquiries we have been able to make, we could never learn any thing else but the following Particulars.

The Ship came to an Anchor to the North of the Lake of the Illinois, where she was seen by some Savages, who told us that they advised our Men to sail along the Coast, and not towards the middle of the Lake, because of the Sands that make the Navigation dangerous when there is any high Wind. Our Pilot, as I said before, was dissatisfy'd, and would steer as he pleas'd, without hearkning to the Advice of the Savages, who, generally speaking, have more Sense that the Europeans think at first; **but the Ship was hardly a League from the Coast,** *when it was toss'd up by a violent Storm in such a manner, that our Men were never heard of since; and **it is suppos'd that the Ship struck upon a Sand, and was there bury'd.** This was a great loss for M. la Salle and other Adventurers; for that Ship, with its Cargo, cost above sixty thousand Livres.*

(A New Discovery of a Vast Country in America — Father Louis Hennepin, 1697)

Summary of Clues: *La Salle and Hennepin deliver the seventh and eighth clues that provide us with navigational data, confirming the sand bar location and that* Le Griffon *was buried among the Huron Islands.*

Clue 7 • *Le Griffon* was only a quarter league from land when the flagship was tossed up by a violent storm.

Clue 8 • *Le Griffon* was driven upon the shallows among the Huron Islands (Big Summer, Little Summer, and Poverty Island).

8-CLUES TO DISCOVERY

Summary

Where the Clues Lead Us

The research of these three primary source documents along with 17th century maps and charts provided the location of *Le Griffon's* resting place. They offer proof to academia, historians, and researchers that this ship went down among the islands at the entrance of Green Bay — *Le Griffon's* elusive Huron Islands. Listed here is a compilation of the final pieces to the puzzle in search of *Le Griffon*.

Clue 1 • La Salle implies that his flagship goes down in the same chain of islands where she had anchored on Washington Island.

Clue 2 • La Salle describes the location having a sandbar that extends more than 2 leagues (1 league equals 2.4 to 3 statute miles).

Clue 3 • La Salle confirms in a letter to his Paris agent that clearly puts the Huron Islands on the Lake of the Illinois — Lake Michigan.

Clue 4 • The 1675 map from La Salle's agent clearly places the Huron Islands between Door County, Wisconsin, and the Garden Peninsula in Michigan.

Clue 5 • The map confirms that *Le Griffon* did not go down among the Beaver Island chain of islands.

Clue 6 • La Potherie's Path Measure of five or six leagues led us to our final search area. It directs us northward to the location of the small bay, Indian encampment and sandbar.

Clue 7 • *Le Griffon* was only a quarter league from land when the flagship was tossed up by a violent storm.

Clue 8 • *Le Griffon* was driven upon the shallows among the Huron Islands (Big Summer, Little Summer, and Poverty Island).

Our search for *Le Griffon* took many years of compiling data. Years were spent in libraries researching and viewing documents. We soon discovered by eliminating the static we could finally see through the layers of misinformation. Above we presented 8–CLUES and in the next chapter we illustrated the navigational paths using maps and charts derived from them. These clues were profound in locating the Huron Islands and provided us a navigational path that lead directly to *Le Griffon's* area of demise — where her final moments were recorded.

La Salle's League

One of the most important factors I had to consider in determining the resting place of *Le Griffon* was to determine the distance of a French league in the 1679 time period, the year when *Le Griffon* disappeared. In France the lieue (league) varied with location and time. I had to decide what measurement of distance La Salle used in his journeys. I like to refer to this distance as a "La Salle League." It is known that in 1674–1793 a league of Paris was equal to 2000 toises (an old French unit of length), or 1.949 meters. 2000 toises equates to 2.4 English statute miles. I, however, had some reservations if 2.4 statute miles to a league was the answer I sought. From my knowledge of navigation principles I was aware of the differences in measurements of terrestrial navigation and nautical navigation. In France the land league equates to 1/25 of a degree (60/25) or 2.4 statute

A New Difcovery of a Large Country in AMERICA by Father Lewis Hennepin

miles and the lieue marine 1/20 of a degree (60/20) or 3 nautical miles which equals 3.45 statute miles. I was aware that during this time the land league was often used in nautical measurements. There is no evidence to determine the exact measurement of distance La Salle was using. Nor can we be certain if the number of leagues quoted as distances in historical documents are accurate. Hennepin stated that *Le Griffon* came to an island at the entrance to the Bay of the Puans (Green Bay), lying **about forty** leagues from Missilimakinak. La Salle himself states a traveled distance of **forty** leagues. While there is little distinction in "**about** 40 leagues" vs. "40 leagues" it still warranted attention. There is little reason to question La Salle's judgment but I had to take under consideration Hennepin's also. To solve this dilemma I took the average of both measurements (2.4 + 3.45). After doing the conversions I arrived at what I had termed a "La Salle's League" to be 2.9 statue miles, rounding off to the nearest whole number, 3 statute miles. It just so happens that the distance from Missilimakinak to Washington Harbor is 120 statute miles, in other words, 40 leagues exactly their traveled distance as noted by La Salle from Missilimakinak to Huron Islands (Washington Island).

In order to know where you're going,
you need to know where you've been.

—Steve Libert

Chapter 6

Liberts' Navigational Path in Search for *Le Griffon*
Derived from the 8–CLUES

It took several years to unravel the clues noted in the previous chapter in drawing our conclusions to the path *Le Griffon* traveled on its return voyage to Niagara. Somewhere along this route she disappeared. Once we discovered the true location of the Huron Islands we began to narrow down the search area. My colleagues and I have been diving among these islands for thirty-five years. We were experienced with harsh weather and understood the storm patterns and water currents in this region. With this extensive experience we became very knowledgeable with all the natural safe anchorage locations among these islands. Our firsthand experience was invaluable.

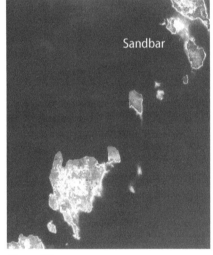

Figure 18

Satellite view of the Huron Islands. Notice the large sand bar far upper right between Big Summer and Little Summer Island.

We detailed our research of *Le Griffon's* last navigational route based on the 8–CLUES gathered from primary source documents outlined in the previous chapter. We begin *Le Griffon's* journey when La Salle departs Missilimakinak (St.Ignace Mission) on September 12, 1679, bound for Potawatomie Island, also referred to as Huron Island, where his cargo of bison and beaver pelts awaits. The following four sequences map out the navigational path *Le Griffon* traveled. These are the last known moments of her mysterious disappearance.

Libert's Navigation Sequence – 1

The First 40 Leagues from Missilimakinak to Potawatomie Island

Present Day Map illustrated by Kathie Libert

Le Griffon sailed 40 leagues to reach her destination of the Huron Islands, a chain of islands that include Potawatomie Island, present day Washington Island (1 La Salle league equals 3 statute miles).

The excerpts that follow tell us that La Salle went to Missilimakinak and would later enter Lake of the Illinois (Lake Michigan), advancing 40 leagues. La Salle advanced as far as the Huron Islands to an island inhabited by the Potawatomie, present-day Washington Island. *Le Griffon* anchored in a deep and protected bay on the northwest side of Washington Island. That bay today is known as Washington Harbor.

La Salle:

> *…he then came and anchored at a place called Missilimakinac, which is the great meeting place of the Outaouas [Ottawa] tribes.*

> *From that place* **he advanced on the Lake of the Illinois as far as the Huron Islands…**

> (1680–82, Claude Bernou from La Salle's Letters)

NOTE: Michilimackinac was often spelled in various ways during the 17th and 18th centuries. i.e.

"Michilimakina" and "Michilimackinak" also "Potawatomie" and Poutouatamis" were spelled differently.

Father Hennepin:

> **Le Griffon** …*sailed into the Lake of the Illinois and came to an Island just at the Mouth of the Bay of the Puans (Green Bay),* **lying about forty Leagues from Missilimakinak;** *It is inhabit'd by some Savages of the Nation call'd Poutouatamis, with whom some of the Men M. la Salle had sent the year before had barter'd a great quantity of Furrs (sic) and Skins.*

(1698, Chap. 22, p. 88)

The following account of Father Hennepin describes the conditions *Le Griffon* was encountering while anchored in Washington Harbor. Hennepin was an eyewitness to the actual events and offers his detailed observations.

Father Hennepin:

> *Our Ship was riding in the Bay,* **about thirty Paces (75 feet) from the furthermost Point of Land,** *upon a pretty good Anchorage, where we rode safely, notwithstanding a violent Storm which lasted four Days. The chief of the Potawatomis seeing our Ship toss'd up by the Waves, and not knowing it was able to resist, ventur'd himself in his little Canow, and came to our assistance. He had the good luck to get safe on board.*

(1698, Chap. 22, p. 89)

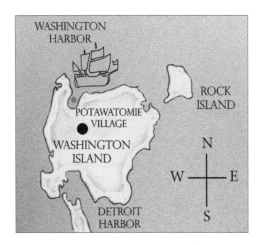

Washington Harbor where Le Griffon *anchored.*

Washington Harbor today. (Photo courtesy of the Door County Chamber of Commerce.)

Washington Harbor, on the northwest side of Washington Island, is 30–80 feet deep and bordered on one side by 100–200 feet cliffs. One could easily anchor 75 feet from the furthermost point of land and still be in the bay. The land, however, obscures the view to the east, west, and the southern quadrants. La Salle believed the winds were favorable for *Le Griffon's* voyage back to Niagara. His official document by Claude Bernou, *Relation of the*

Discoveries and Voyages of Cavelier de La Salle from 1679 to 1681: The Official Narrative, states his observation of the weather the day *Le Griffon* weighed anchor.

La Salle:

> They set sail on the 18th of September, with **a light but very favorable west wind.** What route they took has never been ascertained; and although there is no doubt they were lost, it has been impossible to learn any circumstances of their shipwreck, …

In this next excerpt, Hennepin seemed dismayed that La Salle ordered his ship to sail back to Niagara instead of accompanying them to the south end of the lake.

Father Hennepin:

> **M. de la Salle, without asking any body's advice, resolv'd to send back his Ship to Niagara,** laden with Furrs and Skins to discharge his Debts; our Pilot and five Men with him were therefore sent back, and order'd to return with all imaginable speed, to join us toward the Southern Parts of the Lake, where we should stay for them among the Illinois. They sailed the 18th of September with a Westerly Wind, and fir'd a Gun to take their leave. Tho' the Wind was favourable, it was never known what Course they steer'd, nor how they perish'd;
>
> (A New Discovery of a Vast Country in America)

September 18, 1679, would be the last time La Salle would see his ship, *Le Griffon.* **This is also when the mystery begins: What happened to Le Griffon *and its crew.*

Le Griffon *departing Huron Island on its return voyage to Niagara.*
(Illustration by Kathie Libert)

The Next 5 – 6 Leagues
Le Griffon Faces High Seas and Seeks Shelter

Bacqueville de la Potherie:

Le Griffon...

> *... was driven by a storm into a small bay, five or six leagues from the anchorage which it had left.*

Le Griffon's next leg had the pilot facing heavy residual waves from the previous four-day storm and seeking shelter at Poverty Island, which is five to six leagues from Washington Harbor. Over the course of 35 years, we experienced many severe storms in and around these islands. Many of these storms caused huge, dangerous wave patterns. Even having experienced them firsthand, it was very difficult to see how turbulent the waves actually were when viewing from a leeward direction. One would not see the severity of white water caused by breaking waves as one would from the windward side. From La Salle's vantage point in Washington Harbor, it is highly possible the rough seas from a southerly storm could be obscured from most sides because of the proximity to the surrounding landscape. Only the view looking directly north into open seas would be clearly visible. White water may not be visibly obvious as large waves viewed from a distance often blend in to give the appearance of calm seas. We incurred many southern storms that lasted many days. When these storms subsided — the winds calmed and skies cleared — it usually took one or two days for destructive waves to subside.

> ***White water*** is a sign of substantial height waves, often 3 to 18 feet high. Sailors would refer to gale force winds as storms, often lasting days on the lakes and causing havoc long after the clouds and rain have dissipated.

The Mystery Begins

If one is to question the entry of Bacqueville de la Potherie, in regards to a storm — for what other reason would *Le Griffon* have stopped after traveling only five or six leagues (15–18 statute miles) from where she had just departed? La Salle and Hennepin stated on the 18th of September that the wind was a light and very favorable west wind for sailing to Missilimakinak (St. Ignace Mission). Surely they would have seen or heard a storm approaching 15–18 miles away, but neither source mentions anything about a storm. Either there truly was a sudden storm, or perhaps some other occurrence. The following information is the most important clue that led to *Le Griffon's* resting place. **Potherie said the ship "was driven into a small bay by a storm five or six leagues from the anchorage which it had left."**

> ### Stormy Weather Patterns
>
> There was a four-day storm upon *Le Griffon's* arrival at Potawatomie Island (Washington Island) on September 12th. *Le Griffon* departs with a crew of six on September 18th. On September 19th, La Salle departs late in the evening in canoes from Potawatomie Island and immediately faces another four-day storm. He was concerned for the safety of his ship.

We believe *Le Griffon's* pilot was facing the aftermath of the previous four-day storm in the likes of heavy residual waves.

La Salle could clearly observe that the winds and rain had subsided, but what he could not see, as explained earlier, was the aftermath of the previous storm causing dangerous, residual breaking waves. *Le Griffon's* pilot would have wanted to seek shelter in calm waters to ride out the high seas.

La Salle and his men experienced a second storm while crossing the strait to the mainland in canoes after he left Potawatamie Island on September 19th, the day after *Le Griffon* left. This would be the same storm that caused *Le Griffon's* fate soon after departing Poverty Island. The excerpts below are taken from *Relation of the Discoveries and Voyages of Cavelier de La Salle from 1679 and 1681: The Official Narrative,* pages 47 and 49.

> On the following day, the 19th of September, he pushed forward with fourteen persons in four canoes laden with a forge, with all the tools of house and ship carpenters, cabinet-makers, and sawyers, and with arms and merchandise.
>
> He took his course toward the mainland, distant forty [note: forty here is lost in translation or a misprint and should be four] long leagues from the island of the Pottawattamie's. In the middle of the passage, **there suddenly sprang up out of the deepest calm a dangerous storm, which made him fear for his vessel,** inasmuch as **it raged during four days** with a fury equal to that of the severest ocean storms. Nevertheless he reached land, **where he stayed six days, until the storm was spent.**

Not only has the **GLX's** team personally confronted many severe storms in this region, where it took several days for a storm to become completely spent, we now had supportive historic confirmation that La Salle himself incurred the same aftermath of these storms. *Le Griffon's* pilot departed Washington Harbor not expecting the high seas he encountered. Primary sources suggested that the weather patterns during the time *Le Griffon* was among the Huron Islands were wild and wicked.

In Summary

The pilot sailed out into open seas from Washington Harbor on September 18, 1679, and soon encountered huge and dangerous residual waves. They were driven northward by these southerly waves once *Le Griffon* rounded the leeward side of Washington Island into the open lake. The pilot took refuge from these waves in the lee of Poverty Island. There he would anchor *Le Griffon* in the safety of a small bay. Poverty Island is five to six leagues northeast from the anchorage from where *Le Griffon* had departed.

The north coast of Poverty Island offers great protection from southerly storms and dangerous large waves.

While we had been actively searching for *Le Griffon* for almost 40 years, this was the very same location, for noted reasons, where the **GLX's** team once moored our boats and set up camp for over 25 years while searching for *Le Griffon*. During our many years of exploration, we withstood the most fierce storms from the southern quadrants. Anchoring in this location from storms approaching from the west and northern quadrants can be extremely dangerous. On that note, violent autumn storms often come from the northwest, west, east, northeast, and north, and in that order, can be devastating.

Le Griffon's pilot took refuge from these destructive waves only yards off the north coast of Poverty Island until such a time they subsided. Here, as La Potherie described, is a small bay and, contrary to George Quimby's analysis of Poverty Island in his book *Indian Culture and European Trade Goods,* there does exist a small bay where a ship can anchor safely. The waters are 40 to 60 feet deep and drop off sharply only yards from shore. This anchorage would have protected the ship, as it is in the lee of southerly storms. *Le Griffon* stayed safely anchored there until the next evening, September 19, 1679.

Charles Henriksen's trap net vessel "Karen" moored safely in the small bay off the northern coast of Poverty Island.

Le Griffon is Safely Anchored on the North Coast of Poverty Island and Near an Indian Encampment

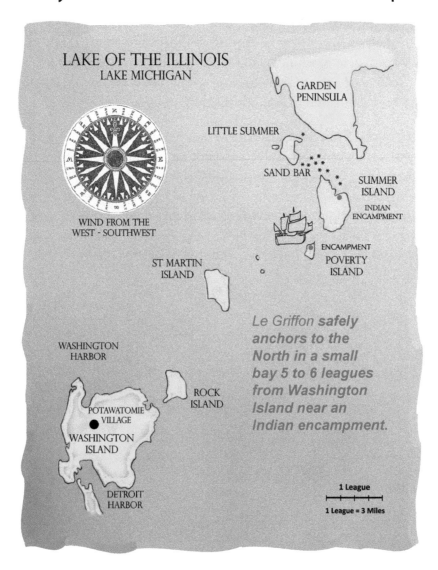

LAKE OF THE ILLINOIS
LAKE MICHIGAN

GARDEN PENINSULA

LITTLE SUMMER

SAND BAR

SUMMER ISLAND

INDIAN ENCAMPMENT

WIND FROM THE WEST - SOUTHWEST

ENCAMPMENT

POVERTY ISLAND

ST MARTIN ISLAND

Le Griffon **safely anchors to the North in a small bay 5 to 6 leagues from Washington Island near an Indian encampment.**

WASHINGTON HARBOR

ROCK ISLAND

POTAWATOMIE VILLAGE

WASHINGTON ISLAND

DETROIT HARBOR

1 League

1 League = 3 Miles

The pilot found safe anchorage on the lee side of Poverty Island where he anchored *Le Griffon* on the northern shore near an Indian encampment. This camp is exactly five to six leagues (15 to 18 statute miles) from Potawatomie Island (Washington Island). The actual distance measured today is 16.5 statute miles. The location of this Indian encampment is an important part of *Le Griffon's* story and offers insight to her disappearance.

The Sequence–3 map shows *Le Griffon's* last safe anchorage. The following excerpts tell the story of *Le Griffon's* final moments after weighing anchor from the safety of Poverty Island. They unravel the mystery of *Le Griffon's* tragic ending among the Huron Islands.

La Salle:

> *...some Indians said that one night they had heard three shots fired by the cannon in the barque, the sound being carried by a strong southwest wind, which was favorable for going past Missilimakinac but not for coming there to anchor.*

What La Salle implies in this excerpt is that there was a native hunting encampment close by. The cannon shots were heard during the evening hours. It is known that the pilot traveled at night, and would usually fire one departing cannon shot before hoisting anchor. La Salle, however, said the Indians had heard three shots. Could this have been a distress signal from *Le Griffon?*

As noted, the Coronelli and Tillemon 1688 map (Figure 19) depicts an Indian encampment either on Big Summer Island or Poverty Island. If one were to examine modern day charts or maps and make a comparison to the 1688 map, they would most likely interpret the symbol for the encampment as being established on the far outer island from the peninsula. This island would be Poverty Island. We, however, are aware that an archaeological discovery of a Native American and Euro-American settlement was excavated in 1968–1970 on Big Summer Island. That site was listed on the National Register of Historic places in 1971, and designated as site 20DE4. It was discovered that the site was occupied during the Middle Woodland (about 100 BC–500 AD), the Upper Mississippian (1000–1500 AD), and Early Historic or Protohistoric periods (1500–1700 AD).

Figure 19
After leaving Huron Island, Potawatomie Village, Le Griffon *anchors safely from torrential residual waves five to six leagues north near an Indian encampment. (For more info on the 1688 map, see page 50.)*

73

It is of the Protohistoric occupancy that caught our attention, as French trade goods were discovered here dating back to approximately 1620 AD.

Our contention was that *Le Griffon* did seek shelter from the dangerous residual waves caused by the previous four-day storm. While moored offshore Poverty Island in a very small bay, a band of native Indians were also encamped nearby. They advised the men of *Le Griffon* of the swift approaching danger. The Indians could see the fast moving southwest storm from their vantage position, unlike the crew of *Le Griffon,* because of the obstruction of the trees where they were so closely anchored.

La Salle's men did not heed the advice of the natives and that evening sailed directly out of sight from the Indians toward a path of certain destruction. They were overtaken by the fierce, unforgiving weather, driving *Le Griffon* northward into harm's way and the deadly shoals. It is said the sound of three shots from a cannon being carried by strong southwest winds were heard by the Indians. We believe these Indians were the same people inhabiting the northeast encampment on Big Summer Island, known present day as site 20DE4.

The key in solving this mystery was La Potherie's path measure which led us directly to Poverty Island **AND** the encampment of the Potawatomie (Pouteatamis). The following is La Salle's and Hennepin's version of what occurred.

La Salle:

> Some Indians, called Pouteatamis, tell me that two days after the vessel left the island where I had quitted here on the 18th of September 1679, this storm arose, of which I have told you: and the pilot, who had anchored with them on **the northern coast, where they were encamped...**

Father Hennepin:

> For after all the Enquiries we have been able to make, we could never learn any thing else but the following Particulars.

> **The Ship came to an Anchor to the North of the Lake of the Illinois, where she was seen by some Savages,** who told us that they advised our Men to sail along the Coast, and not towards the middle of the Lake, because of the Sands that make the Navigation dangerous when there is any high Wind. Our Pilot, as I said before, was dissatisfy'd, and would steer as he pleas'd, without hearkining to the Advice of the Savages, who, generally speaking, have more Sense than the Europeans think at first; but the Ship was hardly a league from the Coast, when it was toss'd up by a violent Storm in such a manner, that our Men were never heard of since; and it is suppos'd that the Ship struck upon a Sand, and was there bury'd.

An old camp found on Poverty Island, most likely a hunting and/or fishing camp. Many of the locals from the Garden Peninsula are descendants of Native Americans and the French. They continue to hunt and fish these islands for a source of food. Pictured is Steve Libert. (Photo by Vance Skowronski, May 1, 1987)

In the late 1980s, we discovered the ruins of an extremely old encampment on the northeast coast of Poverty Island about 40 yards from the water's edge. We often wondered if this was at one time a Native American hunting encampment, and later reoccupied by early European settlers, perhaps as a protective shelter while hunting and fishing. Thirty yards southwest of this camp is a quarter-acre clearing. It is void of trees and consists only of tall grasses. This location today shows many signs of being a deer bedding area. It is the only place on the island, other than the Poverty Lighthouse, completely void of trees and stumps. Could this spot be where the logs for the camp were felled, or perhaps at one time been utilized by native Indians? The Indians hunted throughout these islands and the site appeared to have been untouched by humans for many years. To our knowledge, no archaeological excavation or study was ever conducted on this site.

Metiomek, an Iroquois prophet, placed a curse on the Griffon. Legend says the Griffon "sailed through a crack in the ice," fulfilling the Indian curse.
-- Unknown

The discovery of the hunting encampment found on the 1688 *Partie occidentale du Canada ou de la Nouvelle* map of New France (page 51 and a closeup on page 73), where La Salle had contributed his information, gives credence to Potherie's five to six leagues from where *Le Griffon* anchored after leaving the Potawatomie Village on Huron Island (Washington Island). It is also interesting in that the demise of his ship and crew would come into question as La Salle and the Jesuits began to surmise their own theories to meet their needs. We believe *Le Griffon* sank in a storm, but questions have surrounded the mystery of her disappearance. Did the crew of five plus the pilot not survive the torrential storm described by the Pouteatamis? Could the crew have survived the storm and later been killed? Did the Indians or the pilot burn or sink the ship? Could Indians have captured the crew and held them prisoner? Were the three cannon shots calls of distress? These same questions had probably plagued La Salle in his search for *Le Griffon*.

Many scenarios about the cause of *Le Griffon's* disappearance have persisted. The Jesuits began to believe the Potawatomie were to blame. La Salle distrusted the Jesuits and believed they were trying to have him start a war with them.

La Salle:

The eagerness which I have observed until now in certain persons, to induce me to proceed against the Pouteatami as if they had plundered and burned the barque which was lost on this lake, always made me think there was some mystery concealed under it. I saw no likelihood that Indians could have destroyed the vessel without any remains of it being found anywhere, or anything which had formed part of its cargo being seen in their possession. I was convinced, instead, that the pilot, bribed by someone, had sunk it and had then withdrew, and I could not get rid of that idea, which was founded on a thousand details which would not allow me to doubt it...

(Letter from La Salle to the new Governor La Barre, June 4, 1683)

Father Pierre Charlevoix:

No very authentic tidings were had of it after it left the bay. Some have reported that the Indians no sooner perceived this large vessel sailing over their lakes, than they gave themselves up for lost, unless they could succeed in disgusting the French with this mode of navigating; that the Iroquois in particular, already preparing for a rupture with us, seized this opportunity to spread distrust of us among the Algonquin nations; that they succeeded, especially with the Ottawas, and that a troop of these last, seeing the Griffon at anchor in a bay, ran up under pretext of seeing a thing so novel to them; that, as no one distrusted them, they were allowed to go aboard, where there were only five men, who were massacred by these savages; that the murderers carried off all the cargo of the vessel, and then set it on fire. But how could all these details be known when we are moreover assured that no Ottawa ever mentioned it.

(*History of the Great Lakes, Volume 1*, by J. B. Mansfield, ed.)

Libert's Navigation Sequence–4

Le Griffon Weighs Anchor
The Pilot Ignores Advice from the Native Indians

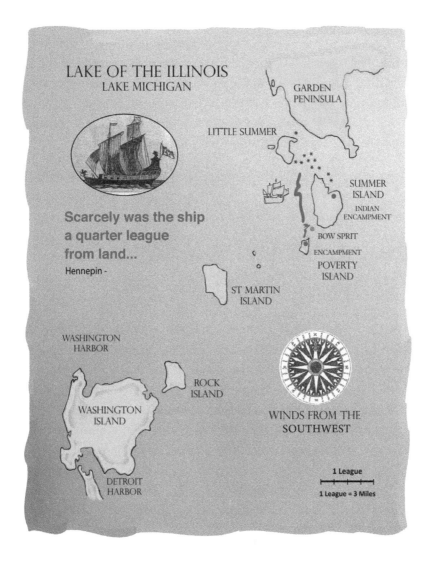

Le Griffon remained safely anchored on the north coast of Poverty Island during the early evening of September 19 as the crew prepared to weigh anchor and resume her return trip back to Missilimakinak (St. Ignace Mission). During this time, La Salle and crew depart Washington Island in four canoes and quickly encounter a severe evening storm. Unknowingly to the crew of *Le Griffon*, the same fierce storm was barreling down upon their position. *Le Griffon,* from its anchorage off Poverty Island, could not see this fast-

approaching storm as it was **obstructed by the land where she was so closely moored.**
The Indians saw this massive storm approaching because they were in a location to clearly
observe it from their vantage point near or on Poverty Island. If on land, the Indians could
have easily trekked to the southeastern side of Poverty Island with a very expansive,
southern-looking view. They certainly would have observed the southerly destruction
heading their way. La Salle encountered the four-day storm late evening, during his
crossing of Porte des Morts (present day Door of Death), south of Washington Island.
The violent weather held him at bay for six days on the eastern coast of the Door County
Peninsula. Storms directly from the north, northeast, south, southwest or southeast could
have kept La Salle confined to these shores. It is plausible La Salle could have continued
his journey had the weather approached his position from the west or northwest. He
would have been in the lee of these storms.

When researching the scenarios of what happened to *Le Griffon*, I considered the
possibilities of a northwest, north, and northeast storm, but immediately ruled those
out as the crew aboard *Le Griffon* would had observed any fast-approaching storm from
these northern quadrants. Keep in mind, *Le Griffon* was anchored very close off the north
coast of Poverty Island and clearly would have possessed a perfect line of sight in those
directions. They would have also have had a direct view of any weather approaching from
the direct west or east while anchored in this small, deep bay.

The Indians warned the crew of *Le Griffon* of the fierce approaching storm. **They advised
the men not to sail towards the middle of the lake, but along the coast, as the sands
made navigation dangerous during any high wind.** The many years of experiencing
severe weather and harsh conditions in this region gave me an advantage into
understanding the very meaning of this passage. I knew where the sands were, as well as
the area referenced as **open lake**. I also understood what sailing along the coast and not
the open lake meant, the coast the Indians suggested *Le Griffon* to sail.

La Salle:

> *...and I may say that the letters which I wrote by the barque on the Lake of the Illinois were the
> cause of its loss, which it would have escaped if I had not delayed it for two days in order to
> complete them with the accounts, maps and memoranda which I wished to send. As the wind
> was very favorable on those two days, it would certainly have got back to Missilimakinak be-
> fore the storm in which, probably, it went down; for as no one in it escaped, and very little of the
> wreckage has been seen, one can only guess.*

(*La Salle's Letters*, page 226 — Margry Translation)

Le Griffon's pilot Luc leaves the safety of Poverty Island's small bay about a quarter of a league from shore. Within minutes the crew faces torrential rains, wind, and violent waves. The ship with its sails furled eventually disappeared from sight. (Illustration by Kathie Libert)

The crew of *Le Griffon* did not heed the advice of the Indians and set sail to the open lake, heading directly for the sands referenced. The same devastating four-day storm that was hammering La Salle was now hammering *Le Griffon* and forcing the vessel northward toward the sands and into shallow waters. This is the exact area Kathie suggested we search 20 years ago. I was skeptical of finding a ship in those shoal waters; however, I finally took her advice and our search plan was revised in 2018. Our concentration pushed further north to search the shallows instead of in deep water.

> *"Take hold,*
> *   this one is breaking over the bow!"*
>
> Steve Libert *(October 2, 1987, storm)*

Summary of Libert's Navigation Research

Le Griffon's Resting Place Among the Huron Islands

Figure 20
Le Griffon's *Navigational Path from Missilimakinak to her final resting place.*

The map in Figure 20 reveals the final navigational path La Salle's ship *Le Griffon* traversed while on Lake Michigan, from Missilimakinak to Huron Island, then inadvertently to her demise among these islands. The location where *Le Griffon* anchored off Washington Island and Poverty Island is based on 40 years of research and diving experience. The map sequences initiated our lifelong quest in search of this fabled vessel. The three islands — Poverty, Big Summer, and Little Summer, kept their secret for over 340 years. Surrounded in mystery and misinformation, the clues were gathered and deciphered, guiding us to the location of the legendary Huron Islands, the area of *Le Griffon's* resting place. With over a dozen unsubstantiated claims to her discovery, *Le Griffon* seems eager to ply the waters once more. Our recent discovery of a colonial-aged shipwreck in the shallows may well bring La Salle's story back into the light.

Like many other maritime enthusiasts, we are patiently waiting for this mythical creature to magically raise her eagle head and lioness body from the depths and continue her voyage. This historical journey and discovery of the Huron Islands may have just solved the Great Lakes most intriguing maritime mystery, *Le Griffon's* final resting place.

Nautical Terms of Interest

Bow: *The forward part of the hull of a vessel or ship.*

Stern: *The back or aft-most part of a vessel or ship.*

Port: *The left-hand side of a vessel when one is facing the front or bow.*

Starboard: *The right-hand side of a vessel when one is facing the front or bow.*

League: *Once used in France to measure the distances on land.*

Knot: *A unit of speed equal to one nautical mile per hour.*

Nautical mile: *A unit of distance used at sea, roughly 2,025 yards English.*

Statute mile: *A unit of distance on land or 1,760 yards English.*

Fathom: *A unit of depth equates to six feet English.*

Hull Speed: *Calculated in knots as approximately 1.34 times the square root of the waterline length of the vessel in feet.*

Leeward: *On or toward the side sheltered from the wind; downwind.*

Lee: *The side sheltered from the wind.*

Windward: *Facing the wind or on the side facing the wind.*

Wind Direction: *The direction the wind is blowing from, i.e., a southwesterly wind would be blowing from the southwest.*

Current Direction: *The direction the current is flowing to, i.e., a southwesterly current would be flowing to the southwest.*

The Huron Islands have a rich history with explorers and fishermen.

Chapter 7

Ships that Disappeared Among the Huron Islands

Separating the Old from the New

There are over 1500 ships known to have been lost in Lake Michigan. One of the first tasks a shipwreck researcher needs to do when searching for new wrecks is to eliminate known wrecks in a targeted area. The shoals among Poverty, Big Summer, Little Summer, and St. Martin islands have already known ship wreckage. Other undiscovered wrecks had to be identified using non-intrusive methods. That usually consists of examining the fastening devices and the construction of the hull. The use of threaded bolts and nuts used during shipbuilding had allowed us to identify 19th and 20th century construction among the ships we discovered.

Shoals and sandbars have taken their toll on ships and lives lost since La Salle's expedition.

When seeking information pertaining to identifying wreck sites and their ages on the upper lakes, we knew that after the loss of *Le Griffon,* there were no other French ships built of size. Navigation had halted after her disappearance, and transportation returned back to the small, flat-bottomed bateaux boats and canoes. In fact, no ship was built on the upper Great Lakes until the British captured Detroit in June of 1761 when the French surrendered all their military and trading posts west of Niagara. By that October, the British had established a shipyard on Navy Island in the Niagara River, close to where *Le Griffon* was originally built. They immediately constructed two, 80-ton schooners called *Huron* and the *Michegon*. The *Huron* would be the first upper-decked vessel built since *Le Griffon*. Also known as the *Gladwyn*, the vessel was wrecked in Lake Erie c. 1770. Lake Erie and Navy Island shipyards marked the beginning of ship construction on the upper lakes. The sloops *Beaver* and *Charlotte*, and the schooners *Boston* and *Victory*, followed and were built and equipped at Navy Island. These vessels were used to explore Lake Erie and its tributaries while providing a garrison to defend the forts from enemies.

Very little is known about early sailing vessels on Lake Michigan. There are accounts of a small primitive barque and barge on Lake Superior by French explorer La Ronde during his copper explorations around 1735. On Lake Michigan, however, there are no records of any decked vessels sailing these waters, and no known shipwrecks recorded. One of the earliest known wrecks above Detroit was the British schooner *Hope*, which wrecked in Lake Huron in 1783. The British had only a few vessels that made reconnaissance trips on Lake Michigan, and none were known to have wrecked there. The *Felicity*, *Welcome*, and *Faith* were said to have patrolled Lake Erie, Lake Huron, and Lake Michigan. The *Felicity*, a one-masted sloop, was discarded and out of service by 1795. *Faith*, a schooner, was wrecked in 1783 in Lake Erie. The *Welcome*, a sloop built c. 1775–1780, supposedly wrecked in a storm at the Straits of Mackinac. Two merchant ships owned by John Askin, the *De Peyster* and the *Mackinac*, sailed Lake Superior. Askin's other vessel *Archange*, a one-masted sloop built in 1774 at Detroit, was also known to have entered Lake Michigan.

Without any known historical records recalling early shipwrecks in Lake Michigan, and the lack of ships traversing the waters, it came down to a simple conclusion. If we were to identify a shipwreck among the Huron Islands that met the criteria of being built earlier than 1800s, it was highly possible that we may have found the fabled *Le Griffon*. To finalize the identification of the wreck, we would have to identify French attributes in its construction versus British. If both criteria were satisfied, there is only one possible ship that falls into this category: that would be Robert La Salle's ship *Le Griffon*. In 2003 and 2013, we had multiple carbon-14 tests performed from prominent AMS laboratories on samples from the recovered bowsprit. Both results concluded a date range of the mid-17th century. These results highly supported our belief that, indeed, the bowsprit was of sufficient age to be that of *Le Griffon*. Carbon-14 dating is not in itself a 100% conclusive tool for determining exact age; however, when collaborated with primary source documents and circumstantial evidence, such as a navigational path that led us directly to the wreck site, the test results provided a strong level of support to our theory.

Shipwreck archaeology began to expand late in the 1960s. Very little was known about sunken shipwrecks until the modern advancement of underwater technologies. It was only then we began to understand early ship construction techniques and the dynamics and processes a submerged or terrestrial shipwreck endures. Our primary goal while observing the wreck was to determine if there were any significant indications on the keel, keelson, bow, timbers, planks, or frames that could direct us or offer a hint as to the origins of the vessel. Is it French- or British-built? We researched early American ship construction to eliminate any contemporary vessels. More importantly, our research focused on understanding French construction techniques, one of the main identifiers in confirming whether or not the wreckage is from *Le Griffon*. We list the key structural differences between French and British design in the next chapter that would later assist us in confirming the wreck's possible identity.

The Huron Islands

Exploring the Islands off the Garden Peninsula

We began to search the Huron Islands' historical past to further understand the boats and ships that traversed the area. I had previously interviewed longtime locals, fishermen, and historians regarding their knowledge and memories concerning any known shipwrecks and the stories related to them. We also referenced a book called *Our Heritage, The Garden Peninsula – 1840-1980*. This book, produced by the Garden Peninsula Historical Society, credited locals and numerous contributors who provided detailed information and the colorful stories that surrounded life on the Garden Peninsula and the surrounding islands. Their rich history also included the mainland town of Garden, the fishing villages of Fairport, Sack Bay, and Fayette — now a State Park. What surprised us most was that by the early 1800s, the islands were inhabited not only by the descendants of the French and native Indians, but also by early settlers who immigrated from Sweden, Denmark, England, Ireland, and Norway, after learning about the water's bountiful fish. Their lives centered on fishing the surrounding waters rather than inhabiting the mainland, which was not even settled until the mid 1850s. The islands off the tip of the Garden Peninsula would become known as some of the best fishing grounds in the north, eventually making the small fishing village of Fairport known for its fish industry.

The Huron Islands have a colorful history. Early explorers, fur traders, French voyagers, and missionaries — such as Father Marquette, who discovered St. Martin Island, sheltered on the shorelines for an overnight stay while traveling between Green Bay and Mackinac. *Le Griffon's* pilot also found refuge among these islands, escaping torrential residual waves from a previous four-day storm. In our research, we discovered that these islands were an important waterway for travelers, not only during La Salle's days, but for the first settlers who came after to make these islands home.

The native Indians fished the islands using gill nets. Father Hennepin referred to them as straight nets. Today these nets are controversial, causing some Native Americans to fight for the rights to fish the area as their ancestors did for hundreds of years. Their current treaty diminished their rights to do so. With conservation and proper management, they hope to regain those rights. One resident in the fishing village of Fairport, among many others, can trace their native Indian ancestry back to Mackinac, Garden, and Grand Blanc islands. Their remarkable stories and history of fishing the old ways are sadly disappearing.

By 1812, fur traders started fishing the surrounding waters off St. Martin Island, finding it a profitable business; and by 1845, a Michigan surveyor discovered on St. Martin permanent settlers who were living there isolated from the world and using their own resources for survival. Before the steam, diesel, and gasoline tugs, the standard fishing boat was the lightweight mackinaw boat with two sails. They were easy to maneuver in and around the islands, and skilled sailors could land them on the rocky shorelines. These 25- to 35-foot fishing boats were numerous around the islands. They had flat bottoms to transport cargo, and took little effort to push up on shorelines for protection and safe storage.

The Summer Islands also attracted fishermen who moved their families there for the summer season, then returned to the mainland. It is said that the term "Indian Summer" derived its name from the native campfires that dotted the shorelines, creating a hazy atmosphere during their hunting expeditions. By the 1870s and 1880s, timber was logged on Big Summer for the furnace operations at Fayette. The lumbermen would stay in the homes built by the early fishermen on the islands. They used wooden barges with flat bows to carry their cargo back to the harbor in Fayette, and the railroad for shipping their products to Escanaba.

Fishermen have inhabited the Huron Islands for over 200 years. Families scoured the shorelines, finding not only fish but ship wreckage along the way. Information found in the materials held by the Garden Peninsula Historical Society Museum helped eliminate wreck sites in our quest in search of La Salle's ship *Le Griffon*. It was noted by historians that any wreck of sizable importance would have been major news to the town folk and recorded appropriately. It is probable that most of these small boats and schooners were eventually disassembled, timbers re-purposed or scuttled in the lake out of the way of boat traffic. The following pages outline interesting historical information on early sailing ships of the past and a list of known wrecks among these islands. We also include the history of known schooners that were built and used by the families that lived in the area.

List of the shipwrecks confirmed to be in the surrounding area:

Poverty Island

Erastus Corning:

A 204-foot schooner that was stranded on the 27th of May, 1889.

Captain Lawrence:

This schooner was stranded on September 19, 1933, and salvaged by locals.

Near Poverty Island

Roen Salvage Barge No. 93:

Sank on October 20, 1969.

Dick Somers:

Sank on November 25, 1877.

Big Summer Island

John M. Nichol:

The steamer was stranded on December 13, 1906.

Mattie C. Bell:

Went ashore on Summer Island with her escort, the steamer James Sherriffs, in a snow storm on October 26, 1895.

C. C. Hand:

The C.C. Hand was bound from Cleveland for Chicago with 24,000 tons of soft coal on October 6, 1913.

Alice B. Norris and Steamer Georgia:

The three-masted schooner Alice B. Norris of 628 tons was built in Milwaukee, Wisconsin, 1872. In 1932, the ship was taken to a bone yard at Sturgeon Bay then to Summer Island for use as a stone dock on the north side. The old passenger steamer Georgia and another unnamed vessel are also submerged in the same area to support the shoreline.

St. Martin Island

E. R. Williams:

This schooner was lost in a storm on September 22, 1895.

Plymouth:

Left Menominee and sank in a storm after being towed by the tug James H. Martin. All lives lost. November 11, 1913.

D. A. Wells:

Skilled ship builders Don and Darius Hazen built the schooner D. A. Wells bound from Escanaba, Michigan to Buffalo, New York. Went ashore on Mile Ground between St. Martin Island and Fisherman's Shoal. Built in 1874 and abandoned 1918.

NOTE: The 420-foot freighter Sinola went aground off Sack Bay, November 11, 1940.

Interesting Historical Accounts among the Huron Islands:

• *Philimon Thompson built the first schooner on Garden Creek in 1866, Homeport, Escanaba, Michigan. He was the first settler on the peninsula and the first to build a sizable two-masted schooner. He launched the boat sideways into the creek using only four pieces of timber. The schooner had a 69′ x 19′ beam. It had a square stern and a plain head. The sawn timbers were purchased from a mill further up the creek. His family lived on Garden Creek and for supplies he would sail to Escanaba. The vessel was named P. Thompson. The schooner was sold the same year it was built and went through five owners, three from Chicago, one in Milwaukee, and the last one from Marquette, Michigan. It was lost sometime after 1870.*

• *Schooners from Mackinac Island came for visits to the islands and would exchange supplies for salted fish cask.*

• *Small sailboats carried people back and forth to Escanaba for entertainment. Many remember sailing there to watch the Ringling Brothers Circus when they came into town. Names of some of the vessels were the* Maywood, Bon Ami, *and the* Saugatuck.

Felicity Log Excerpts
Historically Interesting

1779—Capt. Robertson of the British sloop *Felicity* made a voyage of reconnaissance around Lake Michigan, inducing traders and Indians to support the English.

Felicity, a 45-ton British sloop, built as a merchant craft at the King's Shipyard in Detroit in 1773–74; its sister ship is the *Welcome.* Both ships were owned by Michilimackinac farmer and trader John Askin until the British Navy took possession of them in 1778.

• The ship was armed with four swivel guns, three feet long.
• Patrolled Lakes Michigan, Huron, and Erie to prevent the rebels building boats.
• Patrolled the western shore of Lake Michigan with a crew of eight men, piloted by Captain Samuel Robertson (a U.S. civilian citizen).
• Visited Maskigon (Muskegon) in the fall of 1789.
• The ship's useful life ended in 1796.

Fairport fishing port and docks where **GLX** *managed most of their expeditions with support from Jim Boulley.*

Chapter 8

Three Identifiers in the Search for *Le Griffon*
Location, Construction, and Cultural Artifacts

Many marine archaeologists believe the identity of La Salle's ship *Le Griffon* will be determined by the age of construction. In Lake Michigan, no known ship of significant age is recorded to have been lost. This will make identifying a wreck that is worthy of further investigation less difficult by assessing its fasteners, non-threaded bolts, pit sawn wood, adze marks, hand-forged wrought iron nails, and wooden treenails, also known as trunnels. We did not expect *Le Griffon* to be intact, as we believed she disappeared in a violent storm in a heavily shoaled area.

When we planned an identification strategy, in order to move forward, a wreck site needed to meet three requirements — **location coinciding with historical documents; French construction (Key French Attributes) and age of the ship; and cultural artifacts**. We have provided proof of the location of the Huron Islands in Chapters 5 and 6 through historical documentation. We have also discovered a wreck site that satisfies the criteria of a colonial-aged ship; charted *Le Griffon's* navigational path to her demise, precisely where the wreck was found; discovered old growth timber, non-threaded fasteners and bolts, nails forged of wrought iron, and the fasteners are identical to those found on La Salle's ship *La Belle,* sunk in 1686 in Matagorda Bay, Texas. The evidence by this time looked very promising.

French Construction and Analysis

Le Griffon **was a robustly constructed vessel.**

One of the most important lessons we learned was that nothing of importance would be discovered if all we read and researched was taken literally. The size of the ship La

Salle had built is part of the ongoing mystery surrounding *Le Griffon's* story. In La Salle's papers and manuscripts he references cutting a 42-foot keel when writing to his partners. Twice he referenced this number; once, for constructing his ship *Le Griffon,* and again when referring to building a vessel for sailing down the Mississippi River. What we learned from our discussions with experienced shipwrights, such as Allen Pertner, is that La Salle was most likely requesting an approximate size of vessel that would fulfill his needs for his explorations. La Salle himself was not a shipwright. He did not stipulate as to the precise hull-carrying tonnage of the ship to be built, other than to say about 45 tons burthen. La Salle was also not specific as to the type of vessel to be constructed. He simply referred to building a barque. The term barque (bark) was often used for a nondescript vessel that did not fall into any specific build. Barques were usually small sailing vessels with three masts or sails allowing fewer men to maneuver the vessel. They were commonly built in the shipyards of France. Today, a barque refers to a vessel with a specific sailing arrangement or sail plan.

> ## Notes from a Shipwreck Interpreter
>
> ### The What or Who or is it The Who or What?
>
> A shipwreck interpreter's purpose is not to tell us who a ship is, but instead, to tell us what a ship was. **GLX**, in appreciating the fact that it is not the who, but the what, also feels that in the case of *Le Griffon* the two will be so closely entwined that her identity will become obvious.

Shipwrights were in a league of their own — a creative group of craftsmen much like artists. In conceiving *Le Griffon,* La Salle's shipwright Moïse Hillaret would have constructed a ship using his master shipwright skills, building the size of vessel that would satisfy his employer. Hillaret would first consider his timber resources and the complications of building a vessel in the wilderness and not a shipyard. He and the craftsmen were under extreme danger from the native Indians who wished to destroy *Le Griffon* and do them harm. Hillaret most likely built a shoal draft merchant ship similar to a fluyt with a barque rig — a ship that could carry large loads and was able to be sailed with a small crew.

There were additional considerations for Hillaret. The Great Lakes were uncharted, with treacherous shoals, rocky reefs, strong wind-driven currents, frequent violent storms, heavy fog, and winter ice; all dangerous conditions for sailing. And while not often thought so, the lakes are like a river, flowing from the headwaters of Superior through

La Salle's crew encountered shoal waters and rapids between Lake St. Clair and Lake Huron.

the lower lakes until reaching the Atlantic. Hillaret knew all of this; he also knew his ship would struggle against the current from the moment of her launch, when she would be in danger of being swept over Niagara Falls, and again, when attempting to reach Lake Huron from Lake Erie through the shoals and fast-flowing Detroit and St. Clair rivers. While a strong, steady following wind could carry *Le Griffon* through these places, realistically towing, fending, warping, or kedging that would be required. This is all the work of sailors, but it was Hillaret's job to give them a toughly built ship. *Le Griffon* could not be just another ship.

As an example of how creatively skilled these craftsmen were, shipwrights seldom used or required plans to build their ships. In fact, very few craftsmen were literate. Eventually, the French became one of the first to develop plans (treatises), collaborating with shipwrights and capturing their knowledge on paper to create a standard process for building first-rank warships. This process was obviously still new at the time *Le Griffon* was built in New France. La Salle's ship *La Belle*, built in La Rochelle and wrecked in Matagorda Bay, Texas, was discovered to have over 18 different sets of conflicting specifications in the French *devis*, or register. After excavation it was discovered that most of the recovered pieces consisted of dimensions comparable to the *devis*. However, there were some inconsistencies. A few archaeologists believe these discrepancies may have been the result of the manner and locations in which measurements were gathered. These discrepancies also proved shipbuilding was indeed still a creative process.

Moïse Hillaret was a French shipwright born in 1640 in the parish of Saint-Étienne d'Arvert, between Bordeaux and La Rochelle. He apprenticed in the shipyards of Brouage, present day Heirs-Brouage, while in his teens in the 1650s. He was already a master ship carpenter by the age of 23. Another famous Frenchman, explorer Samuel de Champlain, who founded Quebec and New France on July 3, 1608, also spent his childhood years growing up in Brouage.

Hillaret would have built merchant ships at La Rochelle. There were three basic designs: small, open, square-rigged boats called chaloupes; larger decked or partially decked vessels called barques; and the largest, three-masted ships called pinasses. A highly skilled shipwright and carpenter, Hillaret was asked to become the King's carpenter for New France. He left for Quebec, where he would later meet La Salle and learn of France's Grand Plan to explore the New World. Hillaret is thought to have built the first five ships known on the Great Lakes, some built in collaboration with other shipwrights.

La Salle had three known barques. His third was *Le Griffon*. The smaller ships, *Le Frontenac* and *Le Brigantin*, were open-decked vessels called sloops. Both were twenty-six ton vessels. *Le Frontenac* was built at Fort Frontenac, and La Salle would have acquired it through the sale of the fort. Both *Le Frontenac* and *Le Brigantin* were moored at his fort. *Le Frontenac* was wrecked in Lake Ontario on January 8, 1679. It was a major setback as provisions were aboard for feeding the crew and building supplies for La Salle's third ship, *Le Griffon*, including the iron and anchors. Luckily they were able to salvage most of the iron.

Earlier in December 1678, in their search for a location to build *Le Griffon*, La Salle's barque *Le Brigantin* was anchored overnight in a bay where they sought refuge from chilly high winds blowing over Lake Ontario. The next morning, they discovered her hull locked in ice due to the subfreezing temperatures. The crew had to use axes and knives to chip out their vessel. In the process, they lost an anchor and would later drag the barque on shore to protect it from the lake ice. From there, the men began climbing up along the escarpment of the falls to find the perfect location to establish a shipyard in the wilderness. It is here that La Salle's new, larger barque, *Le Griffon*, would be built.

Hillaret survived the ordeals of exploration. After La Salle's death, Hillaret would spend his remaining years building hundreds of small bateaux plats — boats with flat bottoms and easy to maneuver for local merchants. He was the preeminent boat builder on the lakes at this time.

In our research of ship construction, the particulars of French shipbuilding techniques, compared to the British, consisted of many differences and similarities — with many more similarities than differences. The lack of written knowledge in the industry, and a non-existent recorded history, didn't help in our hopes for a simple "look and see" observation to know whether we were looking at a French or British wreck site. The research was extremely time-consuming. We had hoped that the knowledge would identify the wreck quickly, but we soon realized it was not going to be that simple. At the time *Le Griffon* was built, King Louis XIV's Secretary of State of the Navy, Jean-Baptiste Colbert, was just beginning to standardize the French Navy warships. With no plans or directions on the specifications for the ship — except La Salle's mention of a 42-foot keel timber — shipwright Hillaret would construct a ship he knew how to build utilizing resources he had available.

The earliest materials we found on shipbuilding came from an English seaman employed in her Majesty's Service as a shipwright, William Sutherland, born in 1685 and died in 1740. Like his ancestors, he was a master shipwright in the Royal Navy. Sutherland wrote the earliest known book on shipbuilding in 1711, *The Ship Builders Assistant*. His title was Quality of Master Carpenter for three of her Majesty's Ships, and he was in charge of Inspection and Direction of the work for over 15 years at Portsmouth and Deptford Yards in England.

Another resource we referenced was Blaise Ollivier's *18th Century Shipbuilding: Remarks on the Navies of the English and the Dutch from Observations made at their Dockyards in 1737*. Ollivier was Master Shipwright for the French naval shipyard at Brest from 1736 until his death in 1746. Ollivier was sent to spy on English and Dutch naval shipbuilding, and his remarks provided some important differences in comparing the construction of their first rank warships. Obviously, the time period for both these references comes well after *Le Griffon* was built, and during a time when shipbuilding was changing regularly.

Key French Attributes versus British Construction During the 17th Century

Both resources were insightful on French versus British warship construction, but not for merchant ships. However, we note these differences in the following attributes, knowing they may or may not apply to merchant ships being built at the time. The following list of unique attributes would be used by the **GLX's** team to identify French construction and age of the ship.

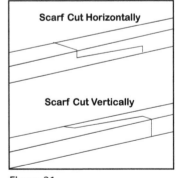

Figure 21

Framing Techniques:

A. Scarf Joints: Horizontal and vertical scarfs are consistently found on both English- and French-built vessels. Sutherland describes English shipwrights as cutting their keelson and keel scarfs vertically. Ollivier mentions that the French cut horizontally (Figure 21). Ollivier's manuscript noted that French shipwrights cut their keels and keelsons horizontally to prevent leakage through the scarf bolts. During Ollivier's observation of English construction, he stated that he noted a few English keelsons cut horizontally. A vertical scarf found in the keel would have been surprising. This was never done by the French, but the English Navy did experiment briefly with vertical keel scarfs, as reported by Ollivier. We do not have a clear view of the wreck's keel, but the keelson is unobstructed and we can clearly see all joints are horizontal scarfs.

B. Framing Techniques: Sutherland mentions that in 1711 the floors and first futtocks in English warship construction were too close together and promoted rot. Air space became essential between the timbers. When *Le Griffon* was built, framing techniques were changing. Our search had focused on archaeological records relating to early 18th century ship hull construction and uncovering any framing trends at the time. There were few records available for the 17th century.

The document, "Eighteenth-Century Colonial American Merchantship Construction" by Kellie Michelle Vanhorn, 2004, provided some interesting information on the evolution of framing ships. It was one area of concern when we first discovered the wreck. The wreck site we believe to be of *Le Griffon* has double-sawn frames. We had thought colonial-age ships were built with single frame timbers. However, through research, we learned that in the late 1660s and early 1670s, nine years before *Le Griffon* was built, an interest in expanding naval architecture began making technical improvements; mainly the use of double frames for the hulls and implementing efficient use of timber. These technical improvements were found throughout the early 18th century. Double-sawn timbers were frequently seen with filler pieces that were placed sporadically, as the carpenter built up from the keel. Interestingly, we did not note any placement of filler pieces at our wreck site. The data researched for framing techniques resulted in no evidence for standardization, other than to save timber and for fast construction.

Frame spacing and dimensions of timbers were also sporadic. Vanhorn noted that the size of the frames usually would match the construction of the vessel. A heavily-built sloop may have had large floors and futtock timbers, whereas another ship had lighter frames, even though its tonnage was over twice the size. The lighter the ship, the less it's cost — yet it retains strength to transport a load of cargo. There were vessels with unevenly spaced timbers between the frames and the dimensions of their thickness varied significantly. The spacing between the frames was generally small, but did vary widely, leading to the conclusion that the framing patterns had not been standardized. Many hulls appeared to be assembled using disarticulated frames, as the timbers did not need to fit closely together. It seemed clear that each floor and futtock set was considered a unit and installed as such and spaced apart as the shipwright determined.

C. Wrought Iron Fasteners: The French were advanced of the English in using wrought iron nails and fasteners, and had experimented with iron knees as early as 1707. In 1670, the English began the practice of utilizing iron in ship construction; however, the quality of iron, the cost of production, a shipwright's tradition, and personal interest slowed the English shipwrights in using iron fasteners in frames. Cast iron was very brittle and subject to fracture, but by 1750, the problem was resolved with new techniques and additives. The French used non-threaded bolts to fasten double-sawn frames together; however, the English used wooden treenails. The English did not practice using iron fasteners until the mid-18th century.

D. Perpendicular Frames: During *Le Griffon's* time, an important French and age-related attribute was the use of perpendicular frames in the bow and stern area. These frames were set at a 90-degree angle from the keel and centerline, extending out to the hull. The timbers supported the curvature of the round bow and the sides of

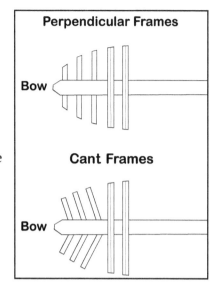

Figure 22

the stern. English shipwrights started using cant frames (as shown in Figure 22) sometime in the 18th century. Sutherland's documents in 1711 make no mention of cant frames. They start to appear in ship models around 1719 and became universal in the 1750s.

E. Stem Scarf: The scarf joint used to connect the stem to the keel and keelson could only be referenced by a few documents available for French construction during *Le Griffon's* time. Plate 3 from the *Album de Colbert, 1670*, gives us an artist illustration of a ship's centerline showing the stem scarf. Shipwrights had several ways of connecting the stem to

Figure 23
Plate 3 from the Album de Colbert, *1670.*

This 17th century French illustration reveals the ship's centerline of the stem, keel, and sternpost configuration nine years before Le Griffon *was built. Moïse Hillaret would have been familiar with this construction while working in France's shipyards. Notice the double-sawn frame amidships.*

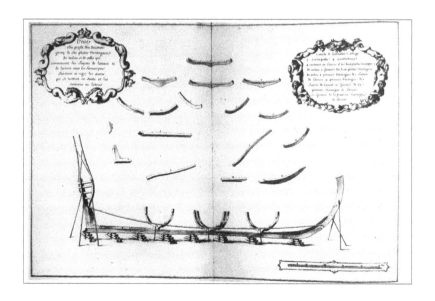

the keel. Some used a forged wrought iron gripe plate, others didn't. We would reference Colbert's illustration (Figure 23) to assist in our identification assessment.

What Type of Ship's Hull to Search For

French maritime history on hull design and construction during the 17ᵗʰ century led us directly to the Dutch. We knew that historically the North American Dutch presence in the mid-Atlantic colonies had flourished around the 1650s in agriculture. These Dutch colonies developed breweries; — trading beer to Marylanders for tobacco — and that they shipped their goods, along with thousands of furs to Amsterdam and beyond. The Dutch had exploited their commercial advantages as early as the 16ᵗʰ century throughout the world, and maintained fierce competition in the merchant shipbuilding industry in America. The English, trying to compete, continued to build heavier ships designed for strength and defense, which meant needing larger crews to sail and more expense. The fluyt hull design significantly elevated the Dutch's commercial capabilities, allowing them to become the world's premier maritime trading nation during the 17ᵗʰ century.

Kathie and I referenced a book titled *La Belle: The Archaeology of a Seventeenth-Century Vessel of New World Colonization,* to better understand French hull design. Allen Pertner had brought to our attention the fluyt, a type of ship originated by the Dutch. With little documentation existing to shed light on 17ᵗʰ century ship construction practices in France, the only materials we had to go on was the *Album de Colbert* from 1670. Within those illustrated plates, we saw a similar Dutch fluyt hull design.

During *Le Griffon's* era of construction, changes to naval technologies were already underway. Jean-Baptiste Colbert, France's Secretary of State of the Navy, had begun to concentrate on infrastructure and dockyards, and then would purchase new ships from the Dutch. The fluyt was a lighter-built cargo vessel with simplified rigging, and the length-to-beam ratios were usually between 5:1 to 6:1, allowing for smaller frames and fewer guns. Merchant ships of all nationalities were designed with the qualities of cargo capacity, small crew size, and maneuverability.

Le Griffon was referred to by La Salle as having a barque rig in his manuscripts, and many fluyt-inspired hulls carried just that rig. This category would have included the fluyt hull design. Since the construction of *Le Griffon* is an important piece of the mystery, it is also imperative to consider how Hillaret would have built a ship — not in a shipyard of France or Quebec — but in the wilderness of upper Niagara above the falls. Some historians have speculated that the ship may resemble the exact size of *La Belle,* but there are many reasons to discount this claim.

At the end of La Salle's 1669–1670 expedition to the Ohio River, La Salle traveled from Lake Erie, up the Detroit River, through Lake St. Clair, and up the St. Clair River by canoe. He understood the limitations of the route from this early expedition. He knew he had to cross rapids on the St. Clair River with some depths of only four feet.

La Salle comments on this part of the navigation:

> The channel between Lake Erie and Lake Huron forms another great difficulty; you cannot make headway against its strong current except with a high wind astern, and **in some places there is only a depth of four feet of water right across**, so that vessels capable of withstanding the storms on these lakes can hardly pass. (Margry II pg 173)

This expedition took place almost nine years before La Salle had his flagship, *Le Griffon,* built. He would certainly have recognized the need to build a shallower draft hull, drafting probably no more than four to six feet of water. If he had followed *La Belle's* formula, a draft of eight feet would have made it impossible to traverse these waters even when being towed by 30 men. Hillaret was aware of these special needs in the construction of the ship. He had already seen the damage ice could do from *Le Brigantin's* unfortunate incident. He knew the severity and destructive nature of the storms and ice flow on the Great Lakes, and that *Le Griffon* would have to withstand storms as violent as those encountered on the oceans. Building the vessel in the wilderness, with unpleasant wintry conditions, also had its own issues. The virgin forests would have provided a variety of old-growth timber unlike that in France, giving Hillaret an abundance of timber resources to complete his task. Montreal's shipyard may have even supplied some cut timbers for master frames and shipped them up-river towards the falls to be carried to the new makeshift Niagara shipyard. There was no shortage of timber to build *Le Griffon*, whereas *La Belle*, built in France in 1684, had timbers that carbon dated to 1474, suggesting repurposed wood. In France, carpenters used repurposed timbers because wood was a scarce commodity in Europe at the time.

As for Le Griffon, it had not yet appeared, and for many months La Salle was heartsick with anxiety for her fate.

We can therefore assume this ship would have been sturdily built and possibly contained unique construction features to maximize cargo, reduce draft, and strengthen structural elements. This is particularly evident in the larger-than-expected size of the keelson and bilge stringers discovered at the wreck site. A stable ship was necessary to prevent the vessel from twisting or compromising any part of the hull during launching and when maneuvering her hull over rocky rapids to and from La Salle's storage facility in Niagara. Large bilge stringers would have been the perfect solution to accomplish this feat.

Cultural Artifacts

Le Griffon was a "Young" Voyager

In reference to cultural materials, we were informed by marine archaeologists that the probability of finding an artifact like a cannon from a wreck site over three and a half centuries old would be highly unlikely. When recalling our legal experiences securing an underwater excavation permit during 2001–2012, we knew that obtaining an archaeological test excavation permit this time around would also be nearly impossible; and without permits, no excavation could be performed. We were reminded by Allen Pertner, however, that the cultural artifact is the wreck itself.

Le Griffon was not operational for any significant time for the crew to accumulate any sizable amounts of personal items. The exact nature of the processes a 340-year-old wreck incurs is not completely understood. These include the actual traumatic wrecking of the vessel and the dispersal of its contents and cultural artifacts over a specific geographic location. It is well understood that heavy items sink to the bottom immediately, while lighter objects are distributed farther from the wreck site, or float away completely. Ship structure, contents, and cultural artifacts often rest directly in plain site on the lake bottom, or are covered by the lake sediments. This, however, may not always be the case. The state in which this vessel lies on the lake bottom is dependent upon the severity of its exposure to environmental conditions over time. These include, but are not limited to: ice, currents, and biological and chemical factors that can enhance or advance the destruction of the wreck. We must also not forget the human factor, meaning salvagers, when it comes to the disappearance or altering of cultural artifacts and ship components. The discovery of cultural materials would definitely assist in identifying the wreck, especially if we were to locate one of the swivel guns or cannons.

La Salle's documents offer some insight into the kind of cultural materials we can expect to find, if any, in and around the wreck site. His first mention of *Le Griffon's* loss is telling and recounts a horrendous ending for his men and his ship. Most items on the ship were perishable. La Salle mentions a few of these items found in the spring after *Le Griffon's* loss among the islands.

> *…Nothing was heard of it until the spring, when **two pairs of linen breeches, spoiled with pitch and all torn, were found on the coast: and finally, this summer, they found a***

hatchway, a bit of cordage and some packets of beaver-skin, all spoiled. *All this made them believe that the barque had run aground somewhere on these islands, and was lost with all that was in it.*

(*La Salle's Letters*, page 226—Margy translation)

Later in his writings, La Salle expands on his list of items recovered to include the door of the cabin and the trunk of the flagstaff. In Claude Bernou's manuscript, *Relation of the Discoveries and Voyages of Cavelier de La Salle from 1679 to 1681: The Official Narrative*, other insights are offered. La Salle's story below describes the events when he sent *Le Griffon* back to Niagara from Huron Island (Washington Island) to pay his creditors with the peltry on board. On page 43 of this document, La Salle's story follows:

On account of the approach of winter, he decided to send back the vessel from this place, and to continue his journey in canoes; but having only four canoes he was compelled to leave in the vessel ***much merchandise and a quantity of utensils and tools of all kinds.*** *All these things he ordered the pilot to unlade at Missilimakinak, where he would get them on his return.* ***He also put on board all the peltry, in charge of a supercargo, and manned the vessel with five good sailors.*** *They had orders to repair immediately to the storehouse which he had built at the end of Lake Erie, where they were to leave the peltry and take on a load of merchandise and other things, to be brought from Fort Frontenac by a vessel which would be awaiting them at Niagara. They were then to sail directly for Missilimakinak, where they would find instructions as to the place for wintering the ship.*

Then on pages 47–49, La Salle describes his loss:

It was not until the following year that M. de La Salle learned all these things. Certain it is that the loss of his vessel cost him more than forty thousand livres, counting not only ***goods, tools, and peltry, but also the men and the rigging which he had brought from France to Canada,*** *and had transported from Montreal to Fort Frontenac in bark canoes — a feat seeming impossible to those acquainted with the fragility of such craft, considering the weight of anchors and cables.*

On the following day, the 19th of September, he pushed forward with fourteen persons in four canoes ***laden with a forge, with all the tools of house and ship carpenters, cabinet-makers, and sawyers, and with arms and merchandise.***

La Salle's men took their own tools with them and continued their journey in canoes. The items left in the hull of the ship were more than likely the items he needed to build his next barque on the Illinois River to continue his expedition to the Gulf of Mexico. That barque was never started.

Final Key French Attributes—Construction Analysis of Wreck Site

When we finished developing the Key French Attributes outlined in this chapter, they would form the criteria **GLX's** team would use to analyze the wreck site. The results of this analysis would determine whether the site was worthy enough to engage a shipwreck interpreter. Through visual observations, we needed to determine any clues suggesting the origin of country and possible age of the site. There is little written information detailing 17th century ship construction. In order to move the project forward, we needed to identify 17th century French and British construction attributes that would assist us in identifying the wreck.

With the following list of Key French Attributes in place as described in this chapter, **GLX's** team began the process to document the wreck site using video, still photography and underwater inspections.

French Framing Techniques:

    A. **Scarf Joints**

    B. **Framing Techniques**

    C. **Forged Wrought Iron Fasteners**

    D. **Perpendicular Framing**

    E. **Stem Scarf**

What Type of Ship's Hull to Search For:

    French merchant vessel, possibly a fluyt approximately 50 to 70 feet long.

The Three Identifiers:

    1) The Location of the Wreck Site

    2) French Construction and Age of the Ship

    3) Cultural Artifacts

We began our assessment of the site to see if we were able to support the second identifier, the origin and age of the ship. If all three identifiers were satisfied, or came close enough to warrant an archaeological investigation, academia will have to consider the possibility of the wreckage resting among the Huron Islands as that of Robert La Salle's *Le Griffon*. Chapter 9 begins with our discovery of the hull, and brings you full circle to a final, exciting result.

Imagine • Explore • Discover
A lifetime of work,
perseverance and love of history.

Chapter 9

Our Story of Discovery

Shifting the Search From Deeper Waters to Shallower Waters

During the entire 2013 Expedition, I was
feeling poorly. I didn't realize at the time I
was suffering from congestive heart failure.
Kathie at first thought I was just stressed,
but I later noticed fatigue, swelling, and
shortness of breath. We knew something
was wrong but I refused to see a doctor until
after the expedition. Ten days later I went
to the hospital in Charlevoix, Michigan,
where doctors informed me that I was
suffering from congestive heart failure caused
by uncontrolled atrial fibrillation (Afib).

A visitor welcomes the divers to show them around.

While living in Virginia the year before, I suffered a pulmonary embolism, resulting in
damage to a quarter of my lung tissue. It would take a year to recover. I decided to take
advantage of the down time and move forward with a total knee replacement caused
by multiple injuries I had incurred many decades earlier as an athlete. Unfortunately,
the surgery didn't go as expected and resulted in some life-threatening complications. I
realized then I was not going to be diving anytime soon and really wasn't sure if I would
ever dive again. It was not a good time in my life.

While recuperating from a disappointing expedition and serious health issues, Kathie
convinced me to search the shallow areas. I could begin this task from the comfort of
our home using my experience and knowledge of satellite imagery. I had been searching
in deeper waters and my initial reaction was that a ship of this size would have been

discovered by now, if indeed it rests in shallow waters. But La Salle's description of the shoals and sandbars extending more than two leagues, La Potherie's path measure, and Hennepin's description stating that the ship was driven upon the shallows and buried in the sand, convinced Kathie where *Le Griffon* rested, and that was in shallow waters. She has always had a gift for solving complex problems by rationalizing the facts and arranging them in an understandable, logical order.

The granular materials of this shoal consist of sand and gravel with some significantly large rocks. From a distance, the shoals often appear to be almost white in color and often protrude above the water surface. The water levels and storms make this area almost impossible to traverse by boat. Even in calm conditions, this region is often impossible to navigate. Kathie believed from the information in primary source documents that *Le Griffon* was within the confinement of the shallow areas of the sandbar. She suspected the French and native Indians were obviously familiar with the area where the ship went down and may have even salvaged portions of it, but nothing has been written or verbalized that would confirm this theory.

While researching the flagship *Le Griffon*, another mystery of interest was researched — the Poverty Island Treasure Legend — a $400 million cache of gold bullion thought to have been lost during the Civil War. The incident supposedly took place on the shoals of Poverty Island. Kathie questioned the possibility of both stories being somehow connected. I believed she could be on to something in her assertion. I had researched the Poverty Island Legend and was able to clarify some of the misinformation. The first was uncovering the correct name of the salvage ship searching for the treasure that unfortunately wrecked off Poverty Island in 1933. The group, using a makeshift

> *"I found it extremely interesting that the* Captain Lawrence *sank on September 19, 1933, and Le Griffon sank 254 years earlier on September 19, 1679."*

diving bell, searched for the five chests of gold from their vessel called the *Captain Lawrence*, to be exact the *Gay Captain Lawrence.* An article had incorrectly referenced their vessel as the *Saint Lawrence*, continuing to contribute to the mystery of the legend as well as the time frame of the war. No records have been found to corroborate the Civil War incident. Once I uncovered the true identity of the vessel, I was successful in locating the only living, surviving member of the crew. I was fortunate to interview this gentleman in person when he was 77 years old. He had been on board the *Captain Lawrence* at the age of 17 in 1932, the year before the ship wrecked. He stated that the skipper of the *Captain Lawrence* was searching the waters for a French-Canadian ship.

He said the story of the legend was passed down to the skipper of the *Captain Lawrence* through many generations. It's quite intriguing, particularity since we know of no other French-Canadian ship that sailed on the Upper Great Lakes other than *Le Griffon*. We wondered if someone salvaged wreckage of *Le Griffon* and was able to identify its French origins. Perhaps *Le Griffon's* story was passed down through generations to this skipper. This was all very interesting, and even possible, especially when you research legends and mysteries and see how stories fold and grow into inspiring tales. If the wreck is *Le Griffon*, this could suggest as Kathie said, the vessel may have been salvaged. The cannon would have had a stamped date and the French fleur-de-lis insignia to identify its origin. This aspect of the story has yet to be investigated.

My recovery from knee surgery would take much longer than anticipated. This gave me ample opportunities to review historical documents and take Kathie's advice to search in shallow waters. I wondered what the chances of locating a shallow water wreck would be by utilizing my knowledge and former experience analyzing sensitive satellite imagery. I knew the exact geographic area to concentrate my search so I began immediately. Remarkably within a just few hours using Google Earth, I detected what questionably appeared to be ship wreckage.

From the day I viewed the image, it would take five years to recover from the complications of health issues before medical doctors hesitantly granted the go-ahead to dive. I was excited to move forward and thought back to my very first dive searching for *Le Griffon* on September 10, 1983. After all the lengthy years of painstaking research, underwater searches, and hardships, was it possible I would be the first person to dive this suspect wreck?

Steve's Discovery of the Hull — The First Dive

Le Griffon, described as a 40- to 45-ton ship, was estimated to be approximately 35 to 70 feet long according to various early historians. The design and construction of the ship's hull and final length was open to interpretation. We believed the structure and specific building characteristics of the wreck would unravel major clues as to the identity of this vessel once we were able to analyze the site.

When the satellite imagery revealed wreckage, we were elated. Kathie and I were still recovering from a disappointing 2013 Expedition that was fresh on our minds. The test excavation revealed no ship beneath the bowsprit as the sub-bottom profiler images depicted. With this new discovery, we were back in the search again, reacquainting ourselves with French and British construction techniques. Analyzing the latest digital image, we began to reassess our research materials, maps, charts, and La Potherie's navigational path. The image showed the location of the wreck positioned in the area deduced from primary source documents. We realized then I may have been searching too far out from the shoal areas. It still seemed reasonable to me *Le Griffon* would rest in deep water, but finally heeding Kathie's advice, I began to search the shoals. My mind echoed sentiments from the past where she had repeatedly told me this for over twenty years. I kept trying to rationalize it in my mind: How can it be that a ship of that size could go undetected for over 340 years in shallow waters? Little did I know there were many reasons *Le Griffon* lay hidden from discovery. And we were about to uncover archaeological evidence of what could be the "Holy Grail" of Great Lakes shipwrecks. I was still in disbelief, not able to even think about the possibility.

Early in the summer of 2018, I was ready to dive. We were lacking our surface support crew member Vance Skowronski who had suffered a minor stroke and was not able to handle the task any longer. With his absence, we were all reminded about our aging bodies and lack of agility. We needed to be careful. Our team focused on an area of the sandbar between Poverty, Big Summer, and Little Summer Islands. I had met with colleagues and brothers Tom and Jim Kucharsky in early June to dive the wreck. Unfortunately, the weather for the week was not cooperating as we incurred gale force winds and dangerous seas. The weather is unpredictable, and it doesn't take much wave action to cancel a whole day, or even a week of diving. It is a slow and encumbering process. The dives were aborted for another time. We usually have a four-month window to make these dives and even then bad weather is always of vital concern. Tom and Jim returned home to Dayton, Ohio, as they had other pending obligations. It wasn't until later when my brother-in-law and surface support crew member Tom D'louhy joined me on location that I could actually dive. The diving operations took place on **Monday, August 20, 2018, at 2:45 p.m**. Temperatures climbed into the 80s and the winds were finally calm. We tracked a course to our GPS coordinates to the exact, suspected location of the wreck while carefully avoiding the shoals.

I piloted the *Grey Lady,* our Achilles SU-18 boat as Tom kept a keen lookout from the bow for shoals and, yes, the wreck. As we approached the location from the north, Tom shouted at the top of his voice, "There it is!" My GPS numbers were spot on. Tom watched the submerged vessel come into view and observed the structure from the deck of our boat. I was in complete awe, especially since I wasn't sure the object detected earlier in the satellite image was even a ship. I couldn't believe it. There lay before us a shipwreck waiting for discovery and it's exactly where Kathie had said it would be. Can this truly be *Le Griffon*? I held my breath.

Steve examines the keelson and frames.
Photo by Rich Gross

A Very Old Shipwreck —
The Elusive *Griffon?*

Tom manned the boat while I dove the shallow waters. Possessing over forty years of diving experience and examining many shipwrecks, it was obvious to me that this ship was old. It is not what I specifically observed in making this judgment; it is what I did not specifically observe. There was a complete absence of any modern day fastening devices. By this I am referring to threaded bolts and threaded nuts. All fastening devices were either wrought iron pinged rods and nails, or wooden treenails. The timbers were pit sawn as evident by the saw marks. The presence of

adze and axe marks were also evident. I found it extremely interesting in the use of wide planking, some measuring 21 inches in width by 1.5 to 2 inches thick, suggesting very old tree growth. The robust size of the keelson was also intriguing. The keelson measured 53 feet in length, sided 10 inches and moulded 11.75 inches with a 6' scarf on the underside. The keelson was constructed from a solid, straight

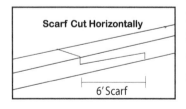

Scarf Cut Horizontally

6' Scarf

piece of oak timber. Two chiseled-out mast steps were observed in the keelson. My first initial assessment of the ship was that it was built sturdily, comparable to a small floating fortress as Hennepin stated.

A significant number of long, thin, tapered wooden poles were observed lying next to the keelson and scattered throughout the wreck site. Kathie believed these to be poles used for fending as the ship incurred shallow waters and rapids. It would later be determined that some of these poles may have also been treenail blanks needed for the construction of La Salle's next vessel. Swimming by the forward starboard side, a gripe plate made of wrought iron is seen in plain view. The plate was attached to the keel just below the keelson (Figure 24). It hung there by one spike. If attached properly, it would be secured to the apron and stem. This dive was getting exciting.

Numerous poles, 3–4 inches in diameter and ranging from 16 to 20 feet long were found on the sides of the keelson.

Figure 24
Forged wrought iron gripe plate attached to the end of the keel. The keel would have been scarfed into the stem.

As I swam, my mind was racing. This ship looked old but just exactly how old? I couldn't shake the fact that I had never heard of this wreck from any of the locals or in my research of known wrecks in the area. We had been diving this area for thirty-seven years and researching and interviewing people even longer. One must realize that Fairport is but a small village built around its fishing industry. When a boat wrecks or disappears, especially with any loss of life, it is not forgotten. I had repeatedly questioned commercial fishermen and many of the locals during these years about lost boats in this region. They had recalled a dozen or so and identified their locations but this specific vessel nor location was ever mentioned. Their parents at the time who were in their 80s could only recall the names of a few lost vessels. They could not recollect any vessels other than the ones already named nor could they remember any from their elders whom I was told also lived into their upper 80s and 90s. One of the people interviewed in the early 1980s lived to the remarkable age of 102. A simple calculation of the math would add up to at least 180 years, meaning that no known shipwreck was ever mentioned, let alone ever discovered, in this area during this time span. One could only imagine my disbelief when wreckage was discovered. The first non-native settlers of Fairport arrived in 1855, although at the time Fairport had no official name. In 1859, a family of fishermen resided on Big Summer Island. As early as 1836, the first Europeans inhabited the various islands — mainly Rock Island, Washington Island, and St. Martin Island. How could it be that this particular vessel had gone unnoticed with a complete lack of knowledge of its disappearance for all of these years? I think it is appropriate to say this ship disappeared at least 180 years ago if not longer. There were no inhabitants other than the native Indians who resided in this region during that time. Although it has been 340 years since *Le Griffon* navigated these waters, what other known ship would had traversed these waters of upper Lake Michigan even 200 years ago?

Figure 25
The stem looking downward toward the knee where the placement of the keelson would have been.

We found the wreck dispersed with four large sections laying in close proximity to each other. Of particular interest was the stem seen in Figure 25. It rests against a submerged,

Figure 26
The forged wrought iron band ends at the stem and keel joint.

ancient, rocky beach partially covered by soccer ball sized boulders. The stem has a thick, forged, wrought iron band that would have extended down below the waterline, ending at the keel and stem joint. The wrought iron band (Figure 26) would have added protection to the bow when plowing through ice, shallow rapids, rivers, or traversing shoal waters around the islands in Lake Michigan. The stem is remarkable. I am reminded of La Salle's ship *Le Brigantin* and the incident of the catastrophic damage done to her hull as the crew cut her free from the freezing water and ice from Lake Ontario. I thought of La Salle's shipwright Hillaret who had to make construction decisions for sustaining a ship of that size. The wreckage was an amazing sight to see, and wished Kathie were here to observe it with me. The age of the ship was clearly making this wreck a real possibility of being *Le Griffon*.

I returned to the forward end of the keelson (Figure 27). Looking towards the keel, I observed the circular wrought iron gripe plate more carefully (Figure 24). The plate was attached to the keel with one spike at the top. There were three spikes missing. The plate would have been attached to the apron and stem. Gripe plates strengthen a ship's bow for any unexpected impacts to the front of the vessel. The keel was observed at the forward end but disappeared under sediment and is obscured by the frame timbers. Overall, what became apparent was the ship's centerline construction, designed for stability. My visual assessment of the ship's size seemed to meet the criteria for an upper-decked vessel of *Le Griffon's* size and construction.

Figure 27
Picture of the keelson looking downward. The forward end of the keelson is built up with deadwood that would coincide with the curvature of the ship's stem.

The end of summer was fast approaching. During the many dives, I took measurements and video recordings of the wreckage. Later that fall, Kathie was able to reconstruct the bow and keelson using rough sketches as seen in Figure 28. They would assist in determining a centerline profile of the ship and help construct the bow, like pieces of a puzzle. She observed that the forward end of the keelson appeared to have butt jointed into a missing apron and stem, indicating the possibility of an older ship. We learned that after the 1750s, English Navy Frigates had extended the keelson timber upwards onto the stem. Although there is an abundance of wreckage to investigate, we realized many components of the ship had not yet been located.

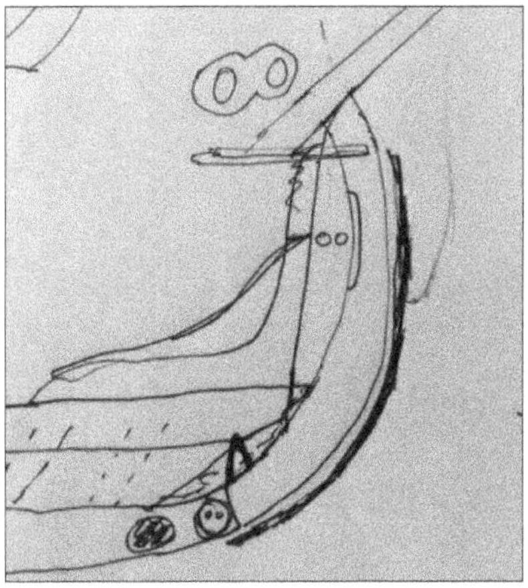

Figure 28
Kathie's rough sketch of the stem connecting the keel and keelson.

At the end of the 2018 diving season, it came to our attention that the location of the wreck site may have been compromised. This is always of great concern for the person leading the expedition. At this point, it became clear to us that we needed to fast track the assessment. **GLX's** team began this process late in the summer, utilizing the Key French Attributes. This initial assessment by the **GLX** team would be an important step in determining if the wreckage was of sufficient age to engage a shipwreck interpreter. It was clear we were on a promising wreck site.

Framing of what is believed to be the starboard side. Notice the wrought iron fasteners covered with quagga mussels.

Hull Analysis — Visual Observation

GLX's 2018 Assessment of Hull — Visual Observation:

To determine if **GLX** needed to engage a shipwreck interpreter, we needed to assess the site by reexamining the images and data gleaned earlier in the summer. The assessment that follows focuses on two areas: the keelson and the bow structure. To date, the stern has not been located. In this initial analysis, we used images to highlight notable areas of the wreck and point out any Key French Attributes and age-related elements. These attributes were used to assess the ship's age and whether they were sufficient to move the project forward.

Overview of Wreck Site

The first visual observation on the keelson was that the ship was constructed for stability and of a size expected for an upper-decked merchant vessel. The French built their merchant ships to carry large quantities of cargo. The keelson's topside revealed that the ship was a three-masted vessel. The forward two steps were mortised into the keelson and the third mast, a mizzenmast, would have rested on the missing upper deck. The ship has large bilge stringers that would have attached to the hull to help shape the sides and offer stability when launched into the water. These timbers would have strengthened the sides of the hull, preventing damage from the pressures of ice, snow, launching, storage, and warping. The hull has a shoal draft for navigating in shallow

waters. The placement of the mast steps and measurements taken from the frames could determine a sail plan as well as provide an illustration by a shipwreck interpreter.

La Salle built a small portage dock on the St. Joseph River and had initially planned to winter his vessel there. After *Le Griffon's* delay of return and with harsh weather approaching, he then planned on wintering the ship at Missilimakinak (St. Ignace Mission). Strengthened ships were used in the early days of exploration especially in arctic areas. After *Le Griffon*, merchant ships were built to transport cargo and were designed more as barges, although large cargo-carrying schooners were also built on the Great Lakes.

Key French Attributes and Age-Related Elements

A. **Scarf Joints.**

Horizontal and vertical scarf joints are consistently found on both English and French vessels. However, the French never used a vertical scarf on the keel. Without a clear view of the wreck's keel, this important attribute is unknown. The keelson, however, is unobstructed and we can clearly observe horizontal scarfing.

Figure 29

The framing timbers seen on what we believe to be the starboard hull appears to have both horizontal and vertical scarfs. Figure 29 shows the frames (ribs) joining another piece of timber. A large knee is also present. Figure 30 shows the joint ends of the timbers missing the attached frames.

The keelson scarf measured 6 feet in length. The missing timber would have been placed under the scarf joint and secured by wrought iron rods. It would have extended to the stern (Figure 31).

Figure 30

We learned that during the 17th century and in earlier construction, these scarfs were cut quite long as seen here. The British began to shorten their scarfs in the mid-1700s to save timber. *Le Griffon,* however, did not have the constraints of timber resources as it was built above the falls using virgin oak.

Figure 31

B. **Framing the Hull. (Figures 32–34)**

As we learned during our research, framing techniques were not standarized during *Le Griffon's* time. English warship construction usually consisted of heavy, tightly spaced frames that eventually promoted rot with little drainage. A merchant ship, on the other hand, had smaller timbers and could carry large tonnage of cargo. Craftsmen would frame their hulls to suit the purpose of the ship, which does not give much indication to the origin of the country in which it was built, other than noting that double-sawn frames were in use at the time *Le Griffon* was built.

Figure 32

As Figure 32 clearly illustrates, pieces of both the port and starboard bilge stringers have survived. These remnants run from their forward point of attachment to the keelson, aft over six frames. And it is only where these short sections of the stringers have survived that we have found some of the ship's frames attached to the keel. Even if these frames have all been broken away at the second futtock, they are invaluable in Allen Pertner's attempt to decipher what he can of the ship's character. But, in addition, the survival of these frames, and the bilge stringers, if only in fragments, gives us an appreciation of how strongly this vessel was built.

Figure 33

The construction and design of this ship is covered more in Allen Pertner's assessment and interpretation of the wreck site.

Figure 34

C. **The bolting of the frames and using wrought iron in construction; non-threaded fasteners.**

The French bolted their frames together using wrought iron. This technique wasn't practiced by the English until the 18th century. Figures 35 and 36 show a considerable amount of erosion between and around the frames; however, you can see the bolts protrude where the wood is missing.

Figure 39 shows a non-threaded bolt with a rove used in the hull construction. Figure 38 shows an 8-inch round gripe plate attached to the keel. It would have been attached to the stem and missing apron under the keelson.

Figure 37 appears to show a notch in the keelson; however, upon further inspection, it is a result of settling of the wreck.

Figure 35

Figure 36

Figure 38

Figure 39

Figure 37

D. **Perpendicular framing of bow and stern.**

When analyzing the keelson's forward end, we discovered the use of perpendicular frames rather than cant frames. As stated before, this is an unique French attribute. Figures 40, 41, and 42 show a close-up of the joints mortised into the keelson to accept the frames. Figure 43 shows the top side of the forward keelson with the mortise joints.

Figure 40

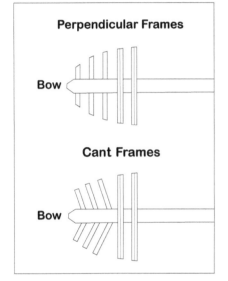

Figure 41

Figure 43

Figure 42

E-a. **Stem construction using Colbert's illustration.**

We began analyzing the stem's scarf joint. As shown in the close-up illustration from the *Album de Colbert, 1670,* in Figure 44, a hooked scarf joint connects the keel to the stem. The scarf found on our stem, Figure 45, had been damaged from the gripe plate as it was torn away from the apron and the stem. However, we were able to distinguish that the scarfs were similar on both the stem and the keel.

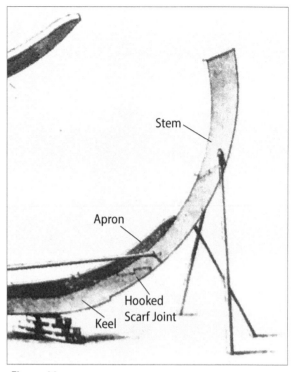

Figure 44

Figure 45

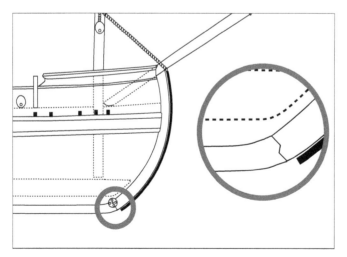

Illustration of the stem's scarf joint on the wreck which connects the stem and keel. The keel's joint was also damaged.

E-b. Stem construction using Colbert's illustration.

The space below the keelson in Figure 46 appears to show a missing apron from the wreckage. This piece would have run up along the inside of the stem as illustrated on page 114, Figure 44. Wrought iron fasteners are still seen under the keelson where the apron would have been secured.

Figure 46

Figure 47

Figure 47 shows the stem structure with white outlines indicating the timber components that are missing and their placement. Notice the large knee that helps support the centerline and stem. These pieces were usually grown or steamed into shape.

Square-pegged treenails were used in 17th century shipbuilding. Notice the square peg inserted into the treenail located on the stem.

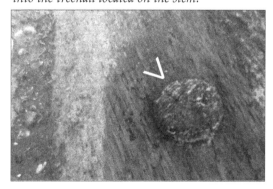

The Search for a Professional Shipwright

In the winter of 2018 after **GLX's** initial assessment, we were convinced the wreck was worthy of further investigation. We needed a professional shipwright who could draw the lines of the ship, determine the approximate age, and help us understand ship construction. We were extremely fortunate the wreck rested on solid bottomlands and was not embedded. Now armed with photos, measurements, and video images, we began our search for the right person. With no permits to excavate from the State of Michigan, we required the expertise of a shipwreck interpreter to conduct a thorough analysis of the site. Before we could request the assistance of the French DRASSM team in identifying this ship, we needed to confirm that it was of significant age. The search for a shipwright would begin from our home in Charlevoix, Michigan.

The Interpreter

In the late fall of 2018, a mutual friend introduced us to a distinguished gentleman, Allen Pertner, who not only had a tremendous amount of experience in designing and building boats but also was a highly experienced technical diver. An expert in cave diving, Pertner had conducted extensive penetrations into Mayan caverns (cenotes) with one of Mexico's leading underwater archaeologists. We were extremely fortunate Pertner resided in Charlevoix. We met at Smoke on the Water, a local eating establishment, for coffee and to discuss our project. Pertner took immediate interest in colonial shipbuilding and was excited about the opportunity to reconstruct the scattered ship components.

Pertner's expertise in shipbuilding allows him to take complex pieces of widely distributed ship wreckage and compile them in a logically assembled composite. He does this by utilizing his talent and skill as a naval architect while possessing exceptional skills and knowledge in ship design and construction. A former submariner in the United States Navy, Pertner is also highly skilled in sailing. He is an avid historian possessing scholarly pre-colonial American information. Pertner's concentration in all these disciplines has made him a valuable asset in Great Lakes Exploration's quest to identify *Le Griffon*.

2019 Expedition

The spring of 2019 began with a team of divers, scientists, structural engineers, and an experienced shipwright stationed on board. Our analysis of the site included the use of remote sensing technology. The sector scan sonar imaging was conducted by Abbott Underwater Acoustics, LLC, the aerial coverage by Eagle Eye Drone Service, and a visual underwater survey of the wreckage by Allen Pertner. Throughout the summer, I was accompanied by my diving partners Jim and Tom Kucharsky and surface support from Dave Butler, Tom D'louhy, and Jim Boulley. It was truly an exciting time of discovery with the usual ups and downs of trying to solve one of the most incredible underwater shipwreck mysteries.

Before the expedition, the team decided it was time to connect with our French colleagues, alerting them that we had found a promising wreck site close to the bowsprit recovered in 2013. We updated their team with some of the initial findings and mentioned bringing on shipwreck interpreter Allen Pertner. Unfortunately, immediately after the discussion, the 2020 pandemic and COVID-19 virus slowed long distance communications. The French dive team schedules were already booked for 2020. The **GLX** team, however, had to push forward. We completed our 2020 dives by the end of summer and immediately began to start the assessment of the site. Pertner would prepare a report of his findings along with a conjectural rendering of the ship based on limited measurements taken earlier in the diving season.

The pandemic complicated the identification of the ship in many ways. The French team needed confirmation that it was *Le Griffon* and we needed a permit from the state to identify the ship. With no permits, we could not identify the site. We were in limbo. It became clear that we had to move the project forward differently as the wreck appeared to have a high probability of being Robert La Salle's ship *Le Griffon*. We decided there was plenty of direct and circumstantial evidence to present our conclusions in a book format. A book would lay out most of our findings in a concise and understandable manner.

Research Suggests a High Probability the Ship is Robert La Salle's *Le Griffon*

GLX's initial goal was to satisfy all three of the established identifiers to confirm identification. Two have been achieved: **the location of the Huron Islands as deduced from historical documents and a list of French construction attributes, particularity the use of wrought iron fasteners.** The third, **cultural artifacts**, would have to wait until we received permits. We are anticipating the French team will find the information in the book compelling enough to take an active role. Even then, they will need to keep an open mind. Early shipbuilding, as they are aware, is still open to interpretation since very little exists in reference materials and the lack of 17th century ship remains for comparison. It would be very easy to get caught up in questions such as: When did double-sawn timbers come into use, or was *Le Griffon* Atlantic- versus Mediterranean-style build? We realized that identifying this ship was not going to be an easy task. Our goal is that the information found in this book will encourage the French to take an active participation in this endeavor.

Below is a summary of the facts that support our suspicions in our belief that we may have discovered Robert La Salle's ship *Le Griffon*:

Location

- Primary source documents, maps, and charts confirm the location of the Huron Islands.

- The geographic location of the sandbar is consistent with the historical descriptions.

Early Construction and French Attributes

- Mixture of wrought iron hand-forged nails, pinged rods, non-threaded bolts, roves and wooden treenails, some square-pegged.

- Saw marks depicting origins of having been pit sawn and adze and axe marks.

- Perpendicular frames used in bow area instead of cant frames.

- The keelson does not extend up the stem.

- Horizontal scarf on keelson. Scarfing on keel is unknown at this time.

- Keel is of oak wood and not elm.

- Stem joint is similar to Colbert's illustration.

- The hull is built with ice-strengthening techniques.

- Thorough investigation into maritime records for this region offers us no known vessel of sufficient age to have wrecked here other than *Le Griffon*.

Cultural Artifacts

- Absent a formal archaeological excavation, we see what appears to be treenail blanks or poles for fending.

Report Analysis

- A report analysis from shipwreck interpreter, Allen Pertner, supports the theory the wreck site appears consistent with the age and construction techniques of Robert La Salle's ship *Le Griffon*.

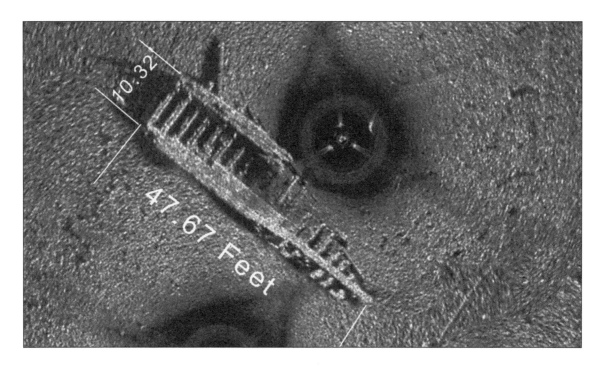

Both images show the same piece of wreckage. Top is a sector scan image. Bottom is a photo.

ANALYSIS

Interpretive Report Introduction

By Allen Pertner, shipwreck interpreter

When I swim through and around a shipwreck for the first time while on an assessment dive, I am always deeply moved. Here or very near here, I always think, this ship and the men aboard her lost their struggle with wind and wave; and all that remains of her, and them, is debris. For me, these wreck sites are sanctified places, and if the Liberts are correct, six men and a boy died here, along with their ship, all of them being victims of an extremely violent fall storm in late September of 1679.

I bring nothing to an assessment dive but a clipboard and a pencil. No camera, no tools, or any preconceived ideas or theories. I am only there to look and I make certain to disturb nothing. I was once a National Speleological Society cave diver, and we had this motto, "Leave nothing but bubbles," and that remains my firm practice.

What am I doing then, if not measuring and taking photographs? I am looking at the debris, looking for some order in the chaos, identifying those timbers I can, asking how she was framed, noting the type of fasteners, trying to get a sense of her hull shape that will in turn tell me what sort of ship she was, looking for manufactured parts, wondering how stiff the hull form might have been, gauging the size of the main timbers and looking in particular for the stem and stern post. This is how it begins in the decipherment of a shipwreck: looking. What I am hoping is that the hull wreckage will give me an insight into what type of ship she was, and an idea as to what she looked like. I do not care who she was, but what she was. A schooner is always a possibility in the Great Lakes, for an example.

But the Liberts do care who she is. They found her, after all, during their decades-long search for the Griffon. The fact the Liberts found this wreck, unknown and un-scavenged, in sight of a busy fishing port with boats coming and going, is an example of a level of determination and perseverance seldom seen in the world of marine archeology. Even today, I find this accomplishment difficult to believe, but as they say, the proof is in the pudding, and the wreck is the pudding.

The truth of the matter is that most wrecks are found accidentally, often by recreational divers, or on occasion by fishermen catching gear on pieces of wreckage, or from a fathometer showing an uncharacteristic object on the bottom, or even sometimes when changing lake currents uncover previously buried portions of a wreck along a shoreline. But the Liberts worked their way to finding their wreck through history, linking together historical waypoints and then following them to the wreck's location. And although they located this extremely old wreck at the end of their Griffon trail, they remain open to the fact that the wreck may actually be the remains of another ship. I see in their openness to the possibility of this wreck having an identity other than that of the Griffon as being professional. There is no group of people so absolutely certain about "what is and what isn't" as the searchers for the Griffon, which is from my point of view, the most unprofessional conduct possible. I have seen in my short time on this job, examples of work from the so called "expert Griffon scholars" where their lack of knowledge of shipbuilding procedures, and their lack of understanding of the correct terminology applied in shipbuilding, as nothing but appalling. The Liberts are the exact opposite of this attitude.

The report that follows this is not only about the assessment dive, but also covers the story of how I became involved with the Liberts, for it is not every day someone knocks on my door about a wreck. Actually, it hardly ever happens, so it tends to get your full attention. Essentially the report leads you through my process of understanding the wreckage enough to be able to conceptually visualize what the ship may have looked like before she was lost, which is what the Liberts asked of me, and more specifically, could she have looked like the Griffon.

There are also some sections that are more general in nature. One of these is questions I have about where the ship was built. Another is about J. Richard Steffy, who to a degree originated this business. I've also included some information about the manner in which I believe Le Griffon was built. And, as usual, there will be some historical diversions that will have found their way into the report — my wife claims these even find their way into my grocery lists — and, last, something called Genetics, which deals with nature of boats.

Remember always, that at this time the wreck lives in a world of the mind, a most changeable place.

Al Pertner

Shipwreck Interpretation

Introduction

Shipwreck interpretation is just another way of saying shipwreck decipherment. And here decipherment means: The act of determining, from a ship's wreckage, always scattered about, in broken disarray, how she was before her violent end. And that, in a nutshell, is what a shipwreck interpreter, or decipherer does; turning back time so we see a ship as she once was.

The qualifications of a shipwreck decipherer are multifaceted. You must be very familiar with the many parts that go together to make a ship, speak the language of ships and sailors, have capacity to see order where there is none, and possess the gift of conjecture and the ability to visualize. It also helps if you have time at sea, under sail, preferably on the open ocean.

A shipwreck interpreter needs to know their history. A sailing ship is only really truly at home when she is at sea, and when she is in harbor at anchor, or lightly tethered at a pier, she seems as nothing more than a temporary visitor, to be gone the next day. But nothing is more intertwined with our world than a wooden ship, and to interpret a shipwreck one must understand that as completely as her construction.

Most important though, would be time spent in the company of, and working with a shipwright of the old ways. A man who lived and breathed ships, a man who was so skillful in working with wood that it seemed like magic, a man who learned to build wooden ships from his father, who, in turn, learned it from his.

A report from a survey by this shipwreck interpreter does not have a standard format, and this report is no different. I include the story of how I came to be involved with the Liberts because it is not often that a present-day shipwreck of sorts leads you to an involvement with another shipwreck that occurred many years ago. And, because this is a little-known business outside of professional marine archeology, I have also included a brief look at the beginning of interpretation work through the person of J. Richard Steffy, the man who originated this field. As an example of the importance of knowing your history, I have pulled into the story, my serious questions about the building site of the La Salle's ship, *Le Griffon*. And it is *Le Griffon*, as they say, that is the gorilla in the room here.

The Beginning

Several years ago, a late summer easterly gale sprung up on Lake Charlevoix, blowing stiffly for several hours. The easterly end of the lake, at Boyne City, with no fetch for the wind had no problems with the gale at all; however, at the western end, near the small northern Michigan town of Charlevoix, things did not go so well. Very quickly, with the east wind blowing over about fifteen miles of open water, a swell started to build. Soon, any boat unlucky enough to be at anchor off the western shore was pitching wildly at its anchor rode. One of those boats was a pretty little sloop named *Sayonara* and at some point, no one knows when, *Sayonara* parted her anchor line and was blown onto rocks, holed and consequently sank.

After the storm, *Sayonara* was removed from the rocks and left sitting on her trailer at water's edge, having been more or less abandoned, with heavy damage over most of her port side, which included a huge hole the size of a dinner plate completely through the hull amidships.

As they say — about me anyway — I don't get out much and as a consequence I knew nothing about any of this, but as they also say, nothing lasts.

Several days later, the easterly gale only a memory now, I was having breakfast at a local Charlevoix restaurant, Smoke on the Water — we call it simply "The Smoke" — when a friend of mine, who worked at the restaurant, told me about *Sayonara*.

"What happened?"

"She blew ashore, on the rocks off Irish during the storm last week."

"Well, that's a bummer, is she bad hurt?"

"Yes, she is, all on the port side, a hole right through the hull you can stick your head through. And the bottom of the keel is all torn up from smashing repeatedly on the rocks. Will you look at her, Al? They are going to throw her away because it is going to cost more to fix her than she's worth."

"Why me?"

"Because, Al, you're the boat whisperer."

Well, boat whisperer was a new one for me, but we did fix *Sayonara,* and my friend, although he knew nothing about repairing a boat so severely damaged, was a great help, and we did the entire job for a miniscule cost. *Sayonara* is still in Charlevoix and if you see her today, you'd never guess she was ever damaged.

Just a few days later, my *Sayonara* friend and I were having morning coffee at the Smoke, when he asked if I'd meet with some friends of his who had some questions about old boats. This is not an unusual experience for me, as I am frequently asked such questions. But when I asked my friend just what type of boat his friends had questions about, he told me he didn't know. I remember thinking how odd that was, that he, a sailor of some experience, did not know what type of boat it was his friends wanted to talk about.

"Schooners, most likely" I volunteered, and hoped. There is nothing to my eye more beautiful than a well-done staysail schooner, and I often picture one in my mind reaching hard pressed through a blue tropical sea, and think, If I had lived my life more smartly, I'd be aboard her right now. It is not lost on me that it was the shipwright Fred Telgard, who, along with my father, recreated in me their love and devotion for ships and the sea. And that the last boat Fred designed and built was a 60-foot staysail schooner, or that many years later I designed a similar boat for Morgan Yacht.

For whatever purpose or reason, I am deeply connected to the past through boats, and over my many years I have learned much about them, some of what is, on rare occasions, actually meaningful. So, I am most times willing to help others with answers or guidance with issues concerning boats and the sea. Or even to just to talk of schooners a bit over coffee at the Smoke.

But it wasn't schooners they wanted to talk about at all.

It was the *Griffon*.

Now, Kathie and Steve Libert are two delightful people: open, friendly, articulate and intelligent. Steve, in person, is a little overwhelming, he resembles what we all think a football player should look like, which in fact he once was. His hands are absolutely enormous as I could not help but notice when we shook hands. Kathie, his wife, is an absolutely charming person, with a warm radiance that is compelling to be around.

But the *Griffon*, come on! No wonder my friend hadn't dared tell me what these people wanted.

For the few that may not know, the *Griffon* was a ship that La Salle, a French explorer, had built in New France to assist in the exploration, or so he said, of the New World. The *Griffon* was lost at sea, or burnt, or buried in sand, or scuttled in 1679 as she attempted to return to Niagara. You get to choose, as no one knows.

Guys like me are always a little leery of the *Griffon* crowd, not that we don't believe she existed, or that she sank. We just see something of Don Quixote in the *Griffon* search, and we are deeply suspicious of the *Griffon* seekers' practice of "forging absolute certainty out a chain of dubious historical facts."

To point, not long before this, two divers in southern Lake Michigan announced that they had found the (umpteenth) *Griffon*, totally failing to note that their supposed 1679 sailing vessel had an engine. Or the Canadian who had **FINDER OF THE GRIFFON** chiseled on his gravestone, completely ignoring the fact that 'his' *Griffon* was built with threaded steel bolts and nuts, totally unknown when the *Griffon* was built.

But in listening to Steve and Kathie, I could not but notice that they were as aware of much of the unreliable and amateurish scholarship around the *Griffon* story as I was. I was impressed, also, by the enormous amount of time they had committed to their effort, decades actually, and that the French government had taken their claims so seriously that they dispatched a team of archaeologists to the area where they were searching. And that Steve, assisted by the French, had recovered a bowsprit that almost certainly came from the *Griffon*.

Then it came: "We feel we have found the *Griffon*. We need some help in identifying some of the wreckage. Would you look at some photographs?"

Steve had taken hundreds and hundreds of photographs of the wreckage, and as soon as he started to show them to me, I could see that this was a very old ship indeed. Everything about it said old. Some of the timbers, like the keelson, were massive, and I knew it would be almost certainly impossible to find such timber today. There were no modern fasteners visible; everything appeared to be hand-forged wrought iron or treenails.

Then something truly remarkable happened. As Steve was showing me how he was able to move the images around, I suddenly saw a letter chiseled into the aft face of a frame; it was the letter "D," the shape of the letter being strongly reminiscent of the "D" you see on a Detroit *Tiger's* baseball cap, just a little more basic in its design. The carving had been done by someone highly skilled with a mallet and chisel. Its precision made me instantly remember the time I had watched Fred Telgard carve documentation numbers into the ketch *Cynthia's* stringer, the precise manner in which Fred's chisel cut into the wood, revealing, in turn and in perfect form, each number and letter. Someone like Fred, superbly skilled, had carved this letter **D**; this wasn't like someone scratching their name on a restroom wall.

"What is that?" I asked Steve. The question wasn't necessary. I was sure I knew.

"Maybe someone carved their initial."

"That's no initial. Look at how skillful and precise the carving is."

From the moment I saw the letter "D" it has felt as if the wreck had touched me. I have been fully committed to the Liberts and their quest since that moment.

Sadly, in the maze of photographs, we have been unable, from that moment to this, to relocate this most important photograph.

J. Richard Steffy

> **THE LOG OF THE SEA OF CORTEZ**, by John Steinbeck:
> *"And a boat, above all other inanimate things,*
> *is personified in man's mind.... man, building*
> *this greatest and most personal of all tools, has*
> *in turn received a boat-shaped mind, and the boat,*
> *a man-shaped soul."*

Richard Steffy was born in May of 1924, in Denver, Pennsylvania. As a young man, he was an indifferent student, and later served time aboard the USS *Wyffels*, DE6, as an electrician's mate. After the Navy, Dick, as he was called, married and started a family, working as an electrician in his brother's electrical contracting company.

But Dick, although he was very skilled, was no electrician at heart. It was just that he was a lot more than an electrician, which in itself is no small thing. If you were to judge him by his indifference to modern education, you would have been terribly wrong. For, as it came to be, Dick wasn't just another person: Dick had a *boat-shaped mind.* As unlikely as it may be, Dick, the indifferent student with the boat-shaped mind, went on to create an entirely new branch of archeology, *the decipherment of shipwrecked hulls.*

Somehow, as he was not as lucky as I was to grow up in a boat yard of the old school, he taught himself about the construction of wooden ships, ships ranging from the c. 2650 BC *Cheops Ship* to ships of the Middle Ages, and all the while, in his basement, he built fully accurate models of these ships, right down to their structural details. So knowledgeable did he become, that in 1985 Dick was awarded a MacArthur Foundation fellowship and, later, he became the Sara W. and George O. Yamini Professor of Nautical Archeology Emeritus, at Texas A&M University and the Institute of Nautical Archaeology.

Being self-educated, Professor Steffy was what is called an autodidact, and as a result of this, he was separate from the normal educational path. None the less, separate or not, he inspired countless marine archeology students over his years, first as a teacher and later in his writings. Not to mention the influence he has had on those of us that shared with him a boat-shaped mind. Professor Steffy died on November 29, 2007.

Navy Island

The first thing you have to do is build it, and you can't just build a ship anywhere. If you were to become interested in the history of the *Griffon* and picked up, for example, the book *Indian Culture and European Trade Goods*, by George Irving Quimby, late of the

University of Washington, or *The Wreck of the Griffon*, by Cris Kohl and Joan Forsberg — both books tell the *Griffon* story — one thing you would read was that she was built on Cayuga Creek. Today, over 300 years later, there are signs claiming to stand on the very spot where the *Griffon* was constructed in the early months of 1679.

But there is a problem with the Cayuga Creek location. The creek was never a part of the original story; in fact, the first mention of Cayuga Creek as being the site of the construction of the *Griffon* did not appear in print until the writings of Henry Schoolcraft in the mid-1800s. This is well over a hundred years after the fact, and Schoolcraft provides us no documentation for his Cayuga claim. But that doesn't seem to matter, because ever since Schoolcraft first mentioned Cayuga as the site, it has become accepted and repeated without question in writings, such as those by Quimby, Kohl, and Forsberg.

Luckily, there are some historical photographs, circa 1880s, of Cayuga Creek that I have had the opportunity to examine and these photographs have caused me to seriously doubt Cayuga Creek as *Griffon's* build site:

- The creek is too narrow, which would have forced a sideways launch, and although a sideways launch is certainly possible, there is no indication in any writings or drawings that this was the case.

- It is of critical importance that the building site, for a ship the size of the *Griffon*, be located on very firm and stable ground to prevent the ship from shifting during construction. In the photographs mentioned earlier, the ground at Cayuga looks unsuitable.

While shipwreck decipherment may not seem to have much relationship to where a ship was built, it is in fact very important. Just knowing where a vessel was constructed can often tell us a lot about the timber that was used, and to some extent, her size.

I propose that the more likely site of her construction was Navy Island, located a short distance from Cayuga Creek. Navy Island also had the added advantage of being more defensible from Indian attack, being that first it was an island, and second, that attacks would require canoes.

An ideal building site for ships would be firm ground, preferably of shale, sloping gently into the water, with an amble stand of timber close by. This may well have been the situation on Navy Island, because a few years after the loss of the *Griffon*, the French established a shipyard on the island where they proceeded to build four ships. After the English drove the French from Canada, they in turn maintained a yard on Navy Island. It is hard to imagine that the crew who were to build the *Griffon* right next door, wouldn't have noticed.

Boat Building in the Woods

Le Griffon came to be because of Moíse Hillaret. He conceived her, selected the timber used in her construction, and prepared the stocks on which she was built. Then, with his crew he built her and when she was complete, he launched and rigged her. They did all of this in less than six months, with hand tools, during the early months of 1679 in what is now New York state.

Hillaret had some direction from La Salle on the type of ship he wanted, for he is believed to have expressed an interest in a barque. And what is a barque? Well, today barque means a particular sail plan — foremast and mainmast, with a lateen rigged mizzenmast. But in Hillaret and LaSalle's time, it more often than not just meant, "a small ship." And a small ship was probably any vessel under 80 feet or so.

There was, however, one other detail La Salle provided Hillaret. LaSalle wanted his ship to have a cargo capacity of about 45 Tuns. 45 tuns is largely a volume measurement, and it is applied to the designated cargo-carrying area of a ship and not just to the total inside volume of its hull. Separate from the cargo capacity then, would be sail lockers, cabins, storage for anchor line, and any other areas needed for the ship and her crew's functioning, and therefore not available for cargo storage.

I know that strikes us as very odd today, when a building contract for a vessel almost 80 feet long would include many pages of material specifications alone. It is difficult to imagine today that a building agreement for a ship could be contained in one single sentence. But that's how it was for a shipwright like Hillaret. And it remained that way for a long time. I have, for example, an actual building contract from 1893 that merely states: "Build me a vessel something like the *Ellen James* with longer masts."

There is one more thing we should consider in addition to interior volume and sail plan, and that is the keel. In much of the *Griffon* literature, the length of the *Griffon*'s keel is most often given as 42 feet or so. And that was certainly possible, surrounded as they were by virgin forest. But there is this to consider. Father Hennepin, the Recollect missionary, writes of being offered the honor of driving the first pin to complete the keel, but declines in honor of La Salle. There is only one place you'd be driving a pin in a keel at this point in building a wooden ship and that is in a keel scarf. And why would you need to scarf a timber for a keel in 1679, when you are surrounded by trees of sufficient length to make a one piece, 40-foot keel? The answer? The keel was longer, maybe in the 60-foot range. And for what it is worth, that is my opinion.

So however long she may have been, where would a shipwright start to build a ship in the woods? First, Hillaret would have made a single amidships frame. He would base its shape on his experience and his understanding of the characteristics that La Salle's vessel would require. He would set this master frame on the ship's keel, exactly amidships. While he had been building the master frame, other shipwrights would have been erecting the stem and stern post and attaching them securely to the keel. Hillaret would now determine his room and space, and begin working fore and aft, building every third frame, shaping each by eye and adze, and attaching each to the keel when it was finished. Next, flexible battens would be run over the outside of the frames that were built and set in place by Hillaret, and the curves developed by these battens were used by other shipwrights to model and build the intermediate frames. This process would continue until the framing was complete. Meanwhile, the rabbet was cut, the frames dubbed, and the ship planked and decked.

And so, it is in this, or other very similar methods, that these unbelievably skilled men like Hillaret, built ships though all the ages that wooden ships were built.

The Liberts' Wreck

What follows is from the log derived from my notes made during the initial dive on the wreck. These notes are general in nature and although taken on site are subject to error. All of this work was done without disturbing the wreckage in any manner.

Figure 1

The wreck lies in water on a largely rocky bottom. The wreck's debris covers a very large area. Scattered about, often at some distance from the principal site, is wreckage that also appears to be from the ship. This material was no doubt dispersed either by a current that runs over the site, or by the action of heavy storms and winter ice. Nonetheless, some sections of the hull, with frames still attached, are visible. The overall appearance, as determined by the wreck's condition, is that this is a very old shipwreck. Present are numerous wrought iron spikes, bent and twisted; unthreaded wrought iron bolts and evidence of treenails, all of which indicate great age.

Keelson

Little of the vessel remains intact, but the keelson, clearly visible, is massive, just under 12 inches square by approximately 54 feet in length. The aft end shows a flat scarf without stop waters, indicating that a part of the keelson had broken free at the scarf. A quick search did not locate the missing section of the timber so even a rough determination of the keelson's length could not be made. No sign of the keel was noted at the aft end of the keelson, but it was clearly visible further forward.

There are two mortised sections in the top surface of the keelson that appear to be part of the masts' steps (Figure 1). It was noted that the section of the keelson adjacent to the aft mast step had been damaged with a significant portion of the keelson's side broken away, as if by great force. Both mortised sections show evidence of missing fasteners, which indicate that the typical built-up steps were in place on this vessel at one time, and the aft, or main mast broke away under force. It was also noted that the forward end of the keelson curved upward a significant degree, and that this was a natural grown shape and was not formed by the builders. The keelson showed no evidence of being notched over the frames, and all fasteners noted on the keelson appeared to be hand forged of wrought iron.

Frames

As mentioned earlier, the wreckage is located in a place where it would have suffered extensive damage during periods of heavy ice. As a result, only six partial frames exist. Not a single frame continues above the turn of the bilge, and most are broken at the middle point of the turn, just enough to give a feeling for how stiff the bilge was. The hull is not flat bottomed, but does have a low deadrise, as indicated by the remaining frames.

The frames are extremely unusual in that they are open. And not open in the typical fashion, where the top timber and the upper futtocks would have been open and the floor members pinned tightly together. Here the frames are completely open and run so over the keel and under the keelson (Figure 2). The frames are treenailed together, so at one time chocks may have been in place between them, though none are in place now, nor is there any evidence that the chocks were ever mortised and pinned (treenailed) in place which was the normal practice. See Figure 9, page 137.

Figure 2

In considering this feature of open frames, I at first wondered if, given all the years that this wreck has sat on the bottom, the frames had just eroded to the point that they began to resemble the "fully" open frames as they appear today. But after time, I decided that the shape of the frames, and the consistency of the inter-open space was just too uniform, and that it must have been a feature of the original construction.

It is very likely that this vessel was constructed during a period of change in the construction of ships, which occurred in the 1600s, although some would suggest in began earlier, in the 1500s. Either way, the result was the same: In a generation or two, ships went from being shell built to plank over frame. And plank over frame is the manner in which this ship was built. Perhaps during this period, totally open frames were tried for a time.

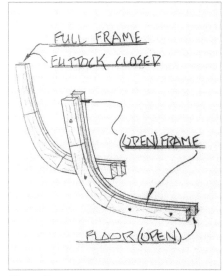

Figure 3

There is one real advantage to a totally open frame, and that is air circulation. Rot is a significant problem in wooden ships, and the French, for example, were critical of the English for placing structural timbers too closely together, which due to the restriction of air movement through the ship promoted rot. Blaise Ollivier, a Frenchman, who was born in 1701 and who became an apprentice shipwright 1715, was a rarity amongst the world's shipwrights as he was literate. And more than just being literate, he also read Latin and knew his Greek, and evidence strongly suggests that he was a highly skilled mathematician as well. Ollivier died young, at the age of 45, but not before writing the book *18th Century Shipbuilding*, in which Ollivier mentions the problem of rot in ships and how the English, as an example, ignored the problem, implying as he did, that the French did not.

Interestingly, Jean-Baptiste Colbert, a French statesman involved in the construction of French ships, published a collection of drawings about boat building, *Album de Colbert,* which has a drawing of a ship's backbone (Plate 3 on page 94) which, if you look closely, shows the master amidship, double frame as being totally open. This is significant, as Colbert was tasked to bring order and standardization to French ship construction and the *Album de Colbert* was a part of that process, which in Plate 3 seems to suggest the use of open frames.

So, in addition to the Liberts' speculation that this is the *Griffon*, there must be added the possibility that we have, as mentioned above, an example of the transition of shipbuilding as it moved from shell built to plank over frame, with shipwrights experimenting with different methods as they moved beyond a method of construction that had been used for thousands of years. And these facts make this wreck doubly intriguing, as the transitional period we have discussed concerning the evolution of shipbuilding rather nicely dovetails with the period of the French shipbuilding in New France.

Bilge Stringers/Half Angle of Entry

The remnants of the port and starboard bilge stringers have survived and remain in place, still firmly attached to the frames. Fortunately, they are of a length that allows a reasonable conjecture as to the fullness of the forward section of the ship. In the beginning there was some concern for how fine the entry was, as suggested by the stringers, which I thought did not agree with the impression I was

Figure 4

getting from the rest of the wreck. It needs to be understood, that older ships would have most likely had fuller lines and therefore larger half angles of entry. I wondered for a time if this was an early wreck of an unknown Great Lakes schooner, for schooners, being fore and aft rigged ships and therefore more weatherly, would have had finer lines as a matter of course.

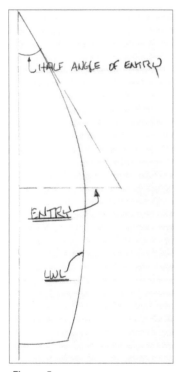

Figure 5

Anyone who has seen the movie *Master and Commander* might remember the captain of the *Surprise* describing his ship as having a "lovely bluff bow." Well, this ship, lovely or not, certainly did not have a bluff bow. In the end, the issue was resolved by Brian Lavery, a leading maritime historian, who laid the quandary to rest by this, and I will quote him: "French ships were regarded as faster with finer lines, which fitted their need to make a quick getaway past the British blockades of their ports. British naval officers loved them." I conclude our questions posed by the half angle of the stringers by the thought that the wreck's entry was far from unusual and was merely a characteristic of the French design philosophy.

I also had access to several sets of lines of French vessels from what I considered to be the same historical period, and it was just as Lavery had claimed — even three hundred years ago the French were shaping ships for speed, maneuverability and the ability to go to weather.

The Bow

I have a rather large library for such a small operation. And in this library is a rather massive book from Texas A&M with the title: *La Belle: The Archeology of a Seventeenth-Century Ship of New World Colonization.* In February 1686, *La Belle*, a small French vessel that had been blown ashore in Matagorda Bay, Texas, was lost. Over three hundred years later she was rediscovered, and the remaining sections of her hull were raised from the bottom of the bay. *La Belle* was buried in mud, which served to preserve much of her hull, and archaeologists from Texas A&M were able to document much of her construction which I now have access to in their book.

I believe *La Belle* to be a contemporary of the *Griffon* (within three or four years), so I used the information available from the work of the Texas A&M archaeologists to compare framing of the two vessels.

I was interested in two areas, the construction of the stem and of the stern post. These are very strongly built and are often the last sections left standing as a boat succumbs to either sea or time. On the Libert wreck, the entire aft end of the vessel has not been found, but the stem and associated timbers were located at the forward end of the keelson. The stem had broken away from keel, keelson, and deadwood and was lying on the lake bottom, in close proximity to the keel.

Figure 7

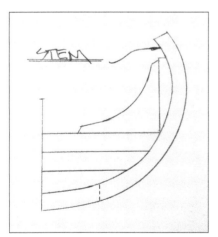

Figure 6

Texas A&M's reconstruction of *La Belle* shows a typical stem, consisting primarily of forefoot, stem, deadwood, and apron. The stem shown is also only slightly curved, bowing only about two French feet over a total length of nearly fourteen feet and is closer to a plumb (nearly vertical) stem than anything else. But in the end, because the stem timber had broken away from the wreck before the wreck was raised, it may have had a somewhat different shape than that shown by Texas A&M archaeologists.

Nothing about the Liberts' wreck looks anything at all like *La Belle*. The stem on the Libert wreck, in comparison, is deeply curved, cut from a single timber, which is in itself remarkable.

To find a timber as deeply curved, and of the size required with the wood's grain correctly oriented, would be an almost once-in-a-lifetime experience for a shipwright. And that fact, in turn, speaks to where and when this ship was built. And that would have been a time before the forests of the Great Lakes had been heavily lumbered and such prized trees as the wreck's stem long gone.

The stem on a ship, along with the keel and stern post, are the first and principal members erected during the building process. All three of these timbers must be extremely strong as they are heavily stressed at times during the life of a ship.

The stern post handles the rudder loads, the keel carries the frames to which the planking is attached (as well of the compression loading from the mast), while the stem deals with rigging loads and the efforts of moving through the sea. The stern post is therefore reinforced during the vessel's construction by *deadwood*, a *deadwood, knee,* and the *inner sternpost.*

The stem, made more complicated if it is deeply curved, is also reinforced. Here we often see a timber called the *apron*, and another very similar in appearance, the *stemson.* These are two very strong yet graceful structural timbers that join tightly to the stem and come together as a single piece, sort of a *stem, apron,* and *stemson* sandwich.

The Libert wreck is completely different.

In Kathie Libert's sketch of the wreck's bow section, there are none of the structural members that I mentioned above. Kathie has drawn the stem (I believe it is more deeply curved than her drawing indicates). as being supported by a knee, with a section of deadwood shaped to pick up the curved inner face of the stem, and with the knee in turn secured to two sections of deadwood that are shown resting on the keel.

The deadwood and the knee supporting the stem, at first, appeared as being out of place, and the whole "affair" looked rather crude. Everywhere else, as I looked about the remains of this ship, I had the sense that she had been skillfully constructed.

There was one other observation that I noted about the structure of the stem's reinforcement; it was much stronger than necessary and, oddly, it seemed in some way to be downwardly orientated. And then, it came to me … ice.

The Libert wreckage is from a vessel that from its very beginning had been conceived to survive ice. In this context, the deeply curved stem (curving almost to the point where it joined the keel), the massive keelson, even the open frames which reduced the length of the unsupported space between frames, made sense.

Ice was a significant factor in the life of ships on the Great Lakes. For the most part, it does not enter into the shipbuilding traditions of England or France, but here in the new world it was a serious issue, and its potential to damage, or even destroy a ship, would have been only too apparent to the shipwrights of Montreal and Quebec. If say, a ship like the *Griffon*, above Niagara Falls, were to survive even a single severe winter of ice in the upper lakes, she would have to take shelter in a navigable river, a river of sufficient size to allow her to get far enough upstream to escape lake ice if it were driven up the river by storms. The ship would have to anchor, or preferably tie off to trees ashore, with her bow upstream and wait the winter out. And if the ship had a curved stem, which would encourage the vessel to rise up in the ice, much in the manner in which modern icebreaker ships are designed to do, and if built with heavily reinforced lower stem and forefoot structure, such a ship could have handily survived any number of Great Lakes winters.

Spars, Sprits, and Steps

In 2013, before locating the wreckage of the hull, the Liberts had located a bowsprit. Of note, the bowsprit was recovered with the assistance of French archaeologists, then documented and attested to by the French archaeologists as being authentic. Eric Reith, one of the French archaeologists who worked with the wreck, created an excellent detailed drawing of the sprit (Figure 8), which years later became a key part of my work with the wreck, while at the same time serving as a real-world model of the value of and need for recording a wreck.

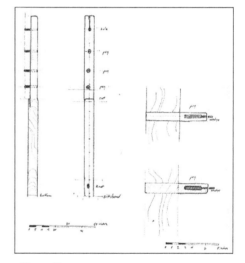

Figure 8

None of the yards, or even masts, have been located by the Liberts, but that is not unusual — none were recovered from *La Belle* either. It is all understandable, for with the somewhat exception of the lower fore and main mast, yards and top masts are not as securely attached to the ship, nor as robust as one might like. But you can always hope, and I always look, for nothing would settle the question of the wreck's identity faster than finding the foreyard, the principal yard on a French vessel.

Genetics

The world into which a ship is first conceived and then born, is everything. A ship's design, her method of construction and even her rig are shaped by her time. The Libert wreck is obviously very old and can only be truly understood if we know some history, history in particular, of the time of her beginning.

We tend to see the history of a particular ship through what we feel her country of origin might be: A French ship is French, and an English ship is English, and, as Rudyard Kipling said, "never the twain shall meet." But that is not quite true. In actuality, a ship can and does show more than just influences from her country of her origin, be she either English or French, for example. There may be well something Portuguese, or Spanish, or Basque, or Dutch, or Scandinavian in her as well. The point here is to understand that only a part of a ship is what we might call "national," much of her is international. There was no single country that dominated the development of ships, they advanced across a broad international front. The men who built these ships were often international in nature themselves, sometimes moving from country to country in pursuit of their vocation.

Think of La Salle's company in New France. La Salle was French, Hennepin was Flemish, his lieutenant and right-hand man was an Italian named Tonti, while the captain of his ship, Luc, was a Dane. It follows that we should not be surprised if he had a Portuguese, Dane, or Basque shipwright helping to build his ship in the woods of Cayuga Creek, or as I think, on Navy Island.

Analysis

I have come to think of this wreck as a new ship for the New World. I see in her what I take as provisions for surviving ice: There is the significant reinforcement of the lower stem and forefoot area, and the deeply curved bow with a wrought iron wrapped stem timber. I have never seen anything approaching this before, and that is not even considering her frames (which if not eroded are fully open), and her large bilge stringers. If for no reason other than these, she should be recorded while it is still possible to do so. This wreck has a lot to say and we should listen. If ever there was, this is the time when we need to remember what Steffy wrote, "Research and reconstruction are contributions, *recording* is a debt."

When the measurement of the bowsprit, the keelson with the mast steps and the stem were put together, a barque rig — foremast, main mast, and mizzen — was a perfect fit. With that information I was able, in an act of conjectural visualization, to develop a rough idea of what the actual length of the ship may have been. And from that, once again depending on the line of a very short section of bilge stringers and the six partial frames, I was able to make an estimate as to its maximum beam. At this point, with the assumption that the shape of the existing frames would have developed in a consistent and predictable manner throughout the ship, I developed a set of conjectural master mold station lines for the ship.

Using this approach, I calculated her dimensions to be (very approximately): LOA 68-70' with a BEAM of 15-16 feet, and DRAFT 5 feet, 6 inches. If the missing section of the keel and keelson were to be found (as these are both substantial timbers they must be nearby), and some remaining sections of the frames documented, it would be possible to reconstruct this ship with acceptable accuracy.

What I developed, through experience and instinct, shows a ship that was fine forward, at least for the time, with low dead rise and a firm turn to the bilge with good form stability. And from what I have available to compare her with, referencing Lavery's comparison of French and English ships, she has a real French flavor.

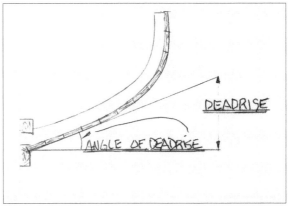

Figure 9

Some may ask: What is the purpose of developing an approximate set of lines, or even a sail plan, on such circumstantial and haphazard evidence? My answer is always the same: Conjecture is what I do, or more correctly, conjectural visualization is what I do. What I see in a debris field is its possibilities. Steffy would have called that a conversation, I don't, but I understand what he meant.

It is not that I at once recognize what is possible, or that what is possible is clear. With the Liberts' wreck, for example, in seeing the angle of entry and the location of the mast steps, I first thought schooner. A schooner and barque have similar fore and aft deck locations for their fore and main masts, so it can be confusing. But when I drew the schooner rig to fit the deck dimension, the main sail was too large.

The possibility of a barque rig is not something you see every day. I would not be surprised, in thinking about the old days, if there was only one barque that sailed on the Great Lakes, and we all know who she was.

So back to the question: What is the purpose of conjecture? My answer is that conjecture is born of imagination, and when joined with a lifetime of living with and thinking of ships and the sea, it is amazing what one can see in a wreck.

But is this the *Griffon*? Of course, this is the big question. And the answer is, of course, we do not know. No one knows. But what do we know? As you have already read this book to this point, you know the Liberts have thoroughly researched the history of shipwrecks in the area where this one is located, and more than that, they have interviewed no small number of people in the vicinity who were in a position to have known of any ship lost anywhere near the wreck site, and the answers were always the same: No. If a ship was wrecked here, it would have had to have happened well before the early 1800s.

So, if not *Le Griffon*, who?

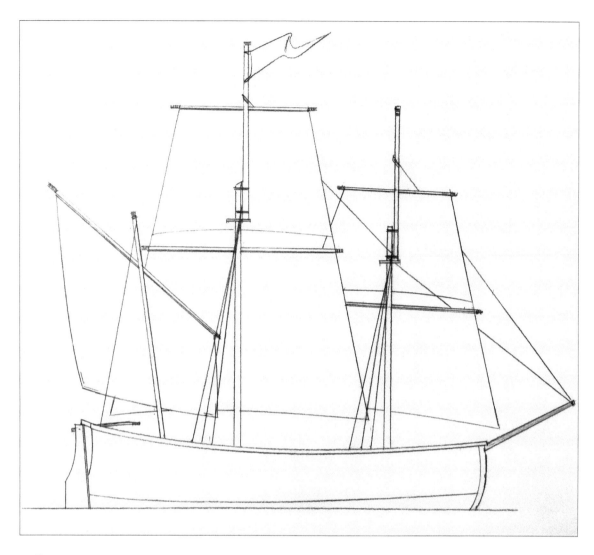

Figure 10

LENGTH: 68-70'
BEAM: 15-16'
DRAFT: 5'6"
(English)

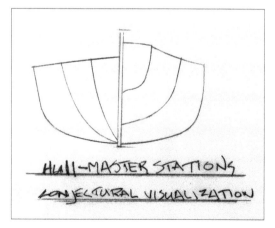

References

Dechene, Louise (1992). *Habitants and Merchants in Seventeenth Century Montreal.* McGill-Queen's University Press.

White, Richard (1992). *The Middle Ground.* Cambridge University Press.

Muhlstein, Anka (1992). *La Salle Explorer of the North American Frontier.* Arcade Publishing New York.

Chapelle, Howard I. (1973). *The American Fishing Schooners 1825 – 1935.* W.W. Norton.

Chapelle, Howard I. (1941). *Boat Building.* W.W. Norton.

Greer, Allan (1997). *The People of New France.* University of Toronto Press.

Greer, Allan (2000). *The Jesuit Relations.* Bedford/St. Martin's.

Fincham, John (1825). *An Introductory Outline Of The Practice of Shipbuilding. Etc.* Kessinger Legacy Reprints.

Biddlecombe, George (1925). *The Art of Rigging.* Echo Point Books.

Black, Conrad (2014). *The History of Canada.* McClelland & Steward.

Lavery, Brian (2017). *Wooden Warship Construction.* Seaforth Publishing.

Smyth, Admiral W.H. (1991). *The Sailor's Lexicon.* Hearst Books.

Quimby, George Irving (1966). *Indian Culture and European Trade Goods.* The University of Wisconsin Press.

Steffy, Loren C. (2012) *The Man Who Thought Like a Ship.* Texas A&M University Press.

Kohl, Cris and Forsberg, Joan (2014). *The Wreck of the Griffon.* Seawolf Communications.

Reminton, Cyrus Kingsbury (1891). *The Shipyard of the Griffon.* Kissinger Publishing.

Hocker, Fredrick M. and Ward, Cheryi A. (2004). *The Philosophy of Shipbuilding.*

De Tonti, Henri (1990). *Relation of Henri De Tonty Concerning the Explorations of La Salle from 1678 to 1683.* Lake Side Press.

Bosscher, Phillip (1992). *The Heyday of Sail, The Merchant Sailing Ship 1650-1830.* Chartwell Books.

Bass, George F. (1972). *A History of Seafaring based on Underwater Archaeology.* Walker and Company.

Bruseth, James (2017). *La Belle: The Archeology of a Seventeenth-Century Ship of New World Colonization.* Texas A&M University Press.

Bruseth, James and Turner, Toni (2007). *From a Watery Grave.* Texas A&M Press

Hundley, Paul Fredric (1980). *The Construction of the Griffon Cove Wreck.* Thesis.

Gardiner, Robert (1994). *Cogs, Caravels and Galleons*. Naval Institute Press.

Nowacki, Horst and Valieriani, Matteo (2003). *Shipbuilding Practice and Ship Design Methods From the Renaissance to the 18th Century.* Max Planck Institute.

Steffy, Richard J. (1994). *Wooded Ship Building and the Interpretation of Shipwrecks.* Texas A&M Press.

Evans, Amanda M. (2017). *The Archaeology of Vernacular Watercraft.* Springer.

Parkman, Francis (1986). *The Jesuits in North American in the Seventeenth Century.* ICGtesting.com
- *Volume 1 Pioneers of Grace in the New World The Jesuits in North American LaSalle and the Discovery of the Great West The Old Regime in Canada.* ICGtesting.com.1986
- *Volume 2 Count Frontenac and New France under Louis XIV. A Half-Century of Conflict Montcalm and Wolfe.* ICGtesting.com 1986

McCarthy, Michael (2005). *Ships' Fastenings.* Texas A&M University Press.

Lacoursiere, Jacques and Philpot, Robin (1992). *A People's History of Quebec.* Baraka Books.

Vanhorn, Kellie Michelle (2004). *Eighteenth-Century Colonial American Merchant Ship Construction.* Texas A&M Thesis.

Adams, Jonathan and Ronnby, Johan (2013). *Interpreting Shipwrecks.* Highfield Press.

Ollivier, Blaise (1992). *18th Century Shipbuilding.* Juan Boudriot Publications.

Cederlund, Carl Olog (1983). *The Old Wrecks of the Baltic Sea.* BAR International Series.

APPENDIX

Glossary of Ship Terms

Adze: Short handled axe with sideways blade; used by boat builders to shape wood

Apron: A timber that fits tightly against and helps support the **stem**

Athwart ships: From one side to another, across the ship

Ballast: Heavy material, such as stone, placed low in a ship to improve stability

Batten: Flexible piece of wood used to determine fairness

Beam: A timber used to support the deck; see **breadth**

Bevel: Curvature of an outer frame surface

Bilge: Interior area of a ship's bottom

Bottom: The submerged portion of a ship's hull

Breadth: The maximum width of a hull; also **beam**

Cant frame: A **frame** mounted at an angle to the **keel** in the ship's ends

Ceiling: Interior planking

Clamp: A ceiling **strake** that provides longitudinal strength to deck beams

Clench: To secure by bending over

Common ceiling: Ordinary **ceiling** used to keep cargo from the **bilge**

Deadrise: How quickly the hull rises up from the **keel** to the turn of the **bilge**

Deadwood: A section of timber used to fill in and strengthen the narrow ends of a ship

Deadwood knee: A **knee** place with **deadwood** to support aft or forward end of a ship

Double frame: **Frames** made in two pairs, bolted together with staggered joints

Double framing: A series of **double frames**

Draft: The amount of water a ship draws

Drift bolt: A metal pin that is driven into a slightly smaller hole

Fine lines: A ship with a fine entry, a low **half angle of entry**

Floor: The area of the bottom of the hull before the turn of the **bilge**

Floor timber: The section of a frame that travels over the **keel**

Forefoot: The curved section between the **keel** and the **stem**, sometimes called the **gripe**

Frame: A timber or assembly of timbers that determine the shape of the hull and to which the planks are attached

Freeboard: Distance between the waterline to the main deck of the ship

Futtock: A section of a **frame** assembly

Garboard strake: The lowest plank on a vessel

Gripe: See **forefoot**

Half angle of entry: A measurement of the fineness of the forward section of the ship

Hanging knee: A grown angle-shaped piece of timber used to support a **beam** at the side of the ship's hull

Hawser: A rope used for towing

Head: The very forward section of a ship

Helm: The tiller or wheel of a ship

Hook scarf: A **scarf** with squared ends that lock it in place

Horseshoe: A horseshoe-shaped plate that is used to bind **stem,** and **forefoot**

Inner sternpost: A **timber** that attached to the inner face of the **sternpost** to strengthen it

Kedge: Small anchor used to move a ship

Kee: Principal fore and aft **timber** that receives **frames, stem** and **sternpost**

Keelson: Internal fore and aft **timber,** that sets on top of the **frames** and attaches to keel

Knee: Holds **timbers** together that meet at angles; an angular grown piece of wood

LOA: Length over all of a ship

LWL: Length of a ship at the water

Lodging knee: A horizontal **knee**

Longitudinal: See **stringer**

Mast step: An assembly that receives the foot of a mast

Midship: Refers to the center of the ship

Midship frame: Widest **frame** in a ship, that prescribes a ship's shape

Mold: A pattern

Molded: Timber as seen from two points of view, the sheer and body

Mortise: A cavity cut into a **timber** to receive a **tenon**

Planking: The outer boards on a hull

Port side: A boat's left side

Rabbet: A groove cut into the **stem**, **keel,** and **stern post** to receive the planks

Rib: Often used incorrectly for **frame**

Ribband: Flexible pieces of wood, sometimes of great length

Room and space: Spacing of **frames** on a **keel**

Rove: Metal washer

Rudder: Used to steer a boat

Scantlings: Important **timbers** on a boat, that are often used in describing their size

Scarf: Overlapping joint in wood

Sheer: Sweeping curve of a ship when seen from the side

Shipwright: Master craftsman

Sided: An unmolded surface

Starboard side: A boat's right side

Stem: The principal upright **timber** at the bow of a boat

Sternpost: Aft vertical **timber** that may receive the planks and carries the **rudder**

Strake: Complete line of planks from bow to stern

Stringer: Longitudinal **timbers** fastened to the inside of the **frames**

Tenon: Carved wooden projection sized to fit a **mortise**

Timbers: In general refers to all members that formed a hull

Top timber: Top section of a sawn **frame**

Treenail: Also trunnel or trennal; round wooded fastening, driven and wedged into place; serves somewhat as a nail

Turn of the bilge: The point where the hull turns up to form the side of a ship

Way: The stocks, or blocks, where a ship is built

MICHILIMACKINAC TIDBITS

Michilimackinac was often spelled in various ways during the 17th and 18th centuries. i.e. "Michilimakina" and "Michilimackinak."

The Ojibwa called the area of the straits Michinnimakinong. In reference to the island itself, the Ojibwa called it "Mitchimakinak" or "Mishimikinaak" for the shape of the "Great Turtle." Michilimackinac today refers to the entire strait that adjoins Lake Huron and Lake Michigan including the Grand Island. Traditionally it referred to St. Ignace Mission, present-day St. Ignace, Michigan.

Mackinaw City and Mackinac Island share the same pronunciation no matter the spelling: Mack-i-naw (as opposed to Mack-i-nac).They are both abbreviations from the Ojibwa word Michinnimakinong. The French later shortened the word to Mackinac and the British to Mackinaw. The island has a large crevice that was used by Native Americans as a specific descriptive identifier for those transitioning the area.

Michinnimakinong is pronounced and translated as follows:
    Mish: Great
    Inni: Connecting Sound
    Maki: Fault
    Nong: Land or Place

Ojibwa is also spelled Ojibwe or Ojibway. They are often called Chippewa, self-name Anishinaabe. The Ojibwa are an Algonquian-speaking North American Indian tribe.

Photos of Discovery
Our Journey of Discovery Through Photos

Double-sawn frames and large bilge stringers. Object on port side of the keelson is unknown.

Forward area of the keelson showing the keel with the attached circular gripe plate.

Rectangular graving piece (filler) on timber.

Close-up of the hand forged wrought-iron gripe plate attached on the keel.

These cultural artifacts may be treenail blanks or poles for fending.

Curved timber and debris lying in an underwater riverbed-like terrain.

Curvature of the frames. The frames are broken at the first futtock.

The placement of the forward and middle mast steps helped Allen Pertner lay out the sail plan for the ship. The main mast step is seen in the photo.

The starboard side of the keelson showing where the forward frames butted.

Allen Pertner inspecting the wreck site.

Angle looking at the bottom of the large knee of the bow section.

The stem with a wrought-iron banding running along the edge.

Close-up of partial frames (ribs).

Planking is seen to the right of the keelson and frames. Many are present underneath a layer of silt.

Portion of the hull section.

Debris field.

Top view looking down on the starboard side of the hull.

Debris field.

Wreckage found in an underwater riverbed.

Repeated intricate cuts on a section of 20-foot piece of timber.

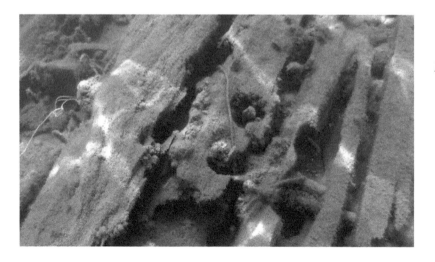

Debris field.

Sector Scan Sonar Images

Produced by Abbott Underwater Acoustics, LLC

Bow portion resting on the starboard side lying against an ancient beach. Note the large knee.

Part of the hull section.

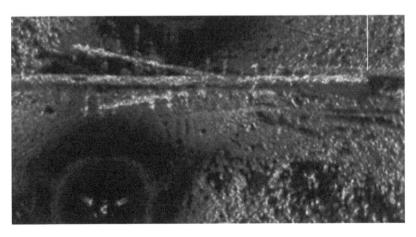

Keelson showing bilge stringers and attached partial frames. Notice the frames and planking under the silt.

Steve and Kathie (Butler) marry in 1981.

Steve heading to Washington, D.C.

GLX's *team and diving colleagues Vance Skowronski, Jim Kucharsky, Tom Kucharsky, and Steve.*

The Early Days

After extensive research on Le Griffon *and the Poverty Island treasure legend, Steve gathered a group of friends to initiate diving activities.*

< Steve and Jim

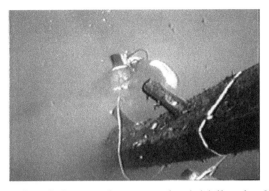

Infrared photography was used to initially take photos of the bowsprit to help penetrate the murky waters.

2013 Expedition. **GLX** *team sets up the boat for the expedition.*

2013 Expedition. Breakfast served to scientists and divers.

Steve and his good friend Dave Parker, founder of Pelican Products.

Steve picking up Parker at his hangar in Charlevoix, Michigan.

Pilot Vance Skowronski with Steve (taking the picture). Departing Michigan's Upper Peninsula headed for the archives in Milwaukee, Wisconsin.

Lenticular cloud over Poverty Island. The area is known for its turbulent weather patterns.

Diving in Lake Michigan off Poverty Island. Carl Carlson, Mike Skowronski, Steve Libert, and Jim Kucharsky.

References

ACUA Underwater Archaeology Proceedings 2014: Article from the 2013 Expedition for Le Griffon.

Album de Colbert, 1670 Plate 3.

America's Louisiana Purchase: Noble Bargain, Difficult Journey. Louisiana Educational Television Authority, 2007. Video.

Bernou, Claude. *Relation of the Discoveries and Voyages of Cavelier de La Salle from 1679 to 1681: The Official Narrative.* 1682, The Translation Done by Melville B. Anderson. (Chicago: The Caxton Club, 1901). Bernou was La Salle's agent in Paris and it is believed his manuscript was written based on La Salle's letters to him.

Brown, Daniel Mark. November 2013. *The Corolla Wreck Exposed: Historical Archaeological Analysis of North Carolina's Oldest Shipwreck,* 1-256 pages.

Flynn, Peter Erik. May 2006. *H.M.S. Pallas: Historical reconstruction of an 18th Century Royal Navy Frigate.* A thesis submitted to the Office of Graduate Studies of Texas A&M University.

Garden Peninsula Historical Society. 1982. *Our Heritage, The Garden Peninsula 1840–1980.*

Goodwin, Peter, February. 1998. *The Influence of Iron in Ship Construction: 1660 to 1830.* The Mariner's Mirror 84 (1): 26–40. Keeper & Curator of HMS Victory, San Francisco Maritime National Park Association.

Hennepin, Father Louis. 1903. *A New Discovery of a Vast Country in America 1697.* Edited by Reuben Gold Thwaites. Chicago: A.C. McClurg & Co. Vol 1. Father Hennepin accompanied La Salle on his journey.

Bruseth, James, Amy A. Borgens, Bradford M. Jones, and Eric D. Ray, eds. 2017. *La Belle: The Archaeology of a Seventeenth-Century Vessel of New World Colonization.* College Station: Texas A&M University Press.

La Potherie, Claude-Charles. *Histoire de l'Amerique Septentrionale or History of Northern America.* (Blair, 1911, I, 353); *Adventures of Nicolas Perrot, 1665–1670,* Louise Phelps Kellogg contributor, 1942.

Mansfield, J. B., ed. 1899. *History of the Great Lakes, Father Pierre Charlevoix, Volume 1.* Chicago: J. H. Beers & Co.

Margry, Pierre. *Decouvertes et Etablissements Des Francais, 1614–1754,* 1876–1879. La Salle's Letters Volumes I and II. Margry was a French archivist and partisan who had private access to the French archives. He came to be the agent of the American historian Francis Parkman. *Journey of M. de La Salle to the River Mississippi. 1680*
Navigation of the Lakes – Geographical Information from Ministere des Colonies.
Amerique du Nord. Enterprises de Cavelier de la Salle C 13 Vol. 3. Fol.33;
La Salle's Letters, Margry Translations 1680-1683

Ollivier, Blaise, 1992. *18th Century Shipbuilding: Remarks on the Navies of the English and the Dutch from Observations made at their Dockyards in 1737.* Translated and edited by David H. Roberts, (1737; reprint, Rotherfield, East Sussex, U.K.: Jean Boudriot Publications, 1992).

Parkman, Francis. *The Jesuits in North America in the Seventeenth Century,* 1867; *La Salle and The Discovery of the Great West, France and England in North America,* 1869.

Perrot, Nicolas. *Memoir on the Manners, Customs, and Religion of the Savages of North America,* in Emma H. Blair, 1911. *The Indian Tribes of the Upper Mississippi Valley and the Region of the Great Lakes,* 1:148, 149n. Cleveland: : The Arthur H. Clark Company.

Quimby, George Irving. 1966. *Indian Culture and European Trade Goods.* Madison: University of Wisconsin Press.

Radisson, Peter Esprit. *Jesuit Relations. 42:219; Voyages of Peter Esprit Radisson, Being an Account of His Travels and Experiences among the North American Indians, 1652 to 1684,* 170 (Boston, 1885).

Sutherland, William. 1711. *The Ship-Builders Assistant.* Reprint 1989. Rotherfield, U.K.: Jean Boudriot Publications.

The Jesuit Relations and Allied Documents – Travels and Explorations of the Jesuit Missionaries In New France, 1610 –1791, Vol. LV, 1670–1672.

Vanhorn, Kellie Michelle. 2004. *Eighteenth-Century Colonial American Merchant Ship Construction.* Thesis, Texas A&M University.

MAPS:

Map– *Bernou, Claude. (ca. 1675)* (La Salle's Agent in Paris) *Research Laboratories of Archaeology: Early Maps of the American Midwest and Great Lakes,* University of North Carolina at Chapel Hill. Reference:
> *[Lac Mitchiganong ou des Ilinois.] [NL catalog attributes this map to Bernou.] [HMC Karpinski series F 29-3-1.] [Service historique de la Défense, département Marine, Cartes et plans, recueil 67, no. 53.] [Formerly in Bibliothèque de la Service hydrographique, 4044B-50.] 1675*

Map– *Franquelin, Jean-Baptiste Louis. (ca. 1650-17..) Research Laboratories of Archaeology: Early Maps of the American Midwest and Great Lakes,* University of North Carolina at Chapel Hill. Reference:
> *[Carte des Grands Lacs.] [Facsimile published as plate 13 in Recueil des cartes, plans et vues relatifs aux États-Unis et au Canada, New York, Boston, Montréal, Québec, Louisbourg (1651–1731), edited by Alphonse Louis Pinart (Paris, 1893). Plate number follows that in Phillips's A List of Geographical Atlases in the Library of Congress, vol. 1, no. 1307.] [HMC Karpinski series F 29-2-1.] [Service historique de la Défense, département Marine, Cartes et plans, recueil 67, no. 43.] [Formerly in Bibliothèque de la Service hydrographique, 4044B-40.]*

Map– *Partie occidentale du Canada ou de la Nouvelle, Coronelli, Tillemon, and Nolin.* (See page 51) American Journeys, Wisconsin Historical Society. www.americanjourneys.org, Reference:

> *This map is a collaboration between Coronelli, Tillemon, and Nolin. It is one of the best representations of the period of the Great Lakes, particularly Lake Superior. Sources for the information shown on the map include Marquette, Joliet, and La Salle. Jean-Baptiste Louis Franquelin, who was based in Quebec and received much of the information brought by the French explorers, was also a significant source of information for this map. This map was number 19 in a made-up atlas, Cartographie du Canada, assembled by Henry Harrisse and later bought by Samuel Latham Brown. It was disbound when purchased and is held separately by the Library.*

DIGITAL RESOURCES:

www.americanjourneys.org, A digital library of early American exploration and settlement. Wisconsin Historical Society.

2013 Expedition. Fox News video of expedition:
https://www.youtube.com/watch?v=e6MYOdM838Q

In December 2005, Steve Libert, president of Great Lakes Exploration Group, LLC, at his home in Oak Hill, VA, with a drawing of the sailing ship Griffon. *Chip Somodevilla, Detroit Free Press*